Metastatic America

Discovering America While Discovering Myself

· ·

A Social Commentary on the State of Race, Religion,
and Culture in the United States as Seen Through the
Life Experiences of a Black Health-Care Executive

· ·

BARRETT BLACKMON

PAGE PUBLISHING, INC.
Conneaut Lake, PA

First originally published by Page Publishing 2021

ISBN 978-1-6624-2722-0 (pbk)
ISBN 978-1-6624-2723-7 (digital)

Printed in the United States of America

PROLOGUE

Let me begin by saying that my book has a nontraditional composition. It is an appealing cocktail comprised of one-part memoir, one-part social commentary, and one-part self-help. It's organized into four sections that mirror the journey of a cancer patient. Prevention, diagnosis, treatment, and survivorship all comprise the cancer experience. There are actions that we can take and behaviors that we can adopt that prevent the onset of disease. Similarly, we can prevent many of the societal ills like racism, bigotry, and hate crimes if we invest in creating opportunities for education and discourse. Proper diagnosis of our problems is key to understand the appropriate course of treatment. Lastly, we need to understand how to move forward and how to survive once we've done the work to address the challenges that we face as a society. It would be wrong to assume that we can open up the conversation to volatile topics and then walk away to leave the impacted individuals without the tools to pick up the pieces and live in a productive and cohesive environment.

Through my life experiences, I illustrate a singular perspective on the American experience. While this perspective is not meant to be comprehensive, my desire is that you find it to be relatable and perhaps translatable. Every reader may not share my exact demographic, educational experience, and socioeconomic position, but the reader may belong to another subset of society that has felt marginalized at some point. Maybe the reader has had challenges in life that have felt insurmountable and could benefit from reading about another train wreck of a life that's working through the restoration process. This book is not designed to provide answers. Unfortunately, I don't have them. Even if I did, you wouldn't take my advice to heart. I've found that the best way to help someone is not by giving them the answers

3

but by helping them to arrive at the right questions. The process of discovering the solution is what encourages growth and wisdom.

My life is a work in progress, and I'm inviting others to travel on that journey of reclamation with me. It's incumbent on all of us to reclaim that which we feel has been lost. Whether it is something material that we at one point had or it may have been a dream that never materialized that we still long to accomplish. Until we've entered the eternal sleep and dirt is shoveled on top of our caskets, reclamation is still a possibility.

PREVENTION
[pre-vent-shen]

Definition: The action of stopping
something from happening or arising

An ounce of prevention is worth a pound of cure.

—Benjamin Franklin

The actions of our yesterday provide the opportunity to prevent the mistakes of tomorrow. Whether they are our mistakes, or the mistakes of others, we can learn a lesson from the past that provides us with a better future.

CHAPTER 1

My Horizon

The World Through My Eyes

"When I grow up, I'm gonna go to work in a suit every day, and I'm gonna make a lot of money!" That's what I told my mom when I was a kid. I had no idea what I would do or how I would get there, but I knew that people were often identified by their occupation. This was especially a stretch since the only rich people I knew were on television and the only time I wore a suit was for "Easter Sunday." I needed to find a mentor or a role model, so I would ask random people, "So what do you do for a living?" That's a common icebreaker because (1) it gets a person to talk about himself, which most people love to do, and (2) it provides a little bit of insight about the personality of the person. For example, if someone says they're a doctor, you may think that she either has a passion for helping people who are in need or has a propensity to understand complex systems. If someone tells you that they're a mechanic, you may think that they're gifted with their hands and have the ability to troubleshoot problems efficiently with limited information. Even a transitionary or part-time job says something about a person's natural affinity. Sometimes, you can just meet a person and guess what kind of work they do before they tell you.

The first time I met the guy who would become one of my professional mentors, thirty years after that conversation with my mom, I remember being able to clearly see why he was a successful lawyer. He was a native Texan with a larger-than-life swagger and slight Southern drawl that presented as assured confidence, not simpleton hospitality. Our mentoring sessions were what I can assume would have been similar to having a conversation with Jesus. No, I had no misperceptions about him being my messiah, but his cadence of speech and ability to tell a story could raise an audience from the dead. I'd ask Dan a question, and he'd lean back in his chair; tilt his head to one side, providing a pensive expression along the way; and then launch into a monologue filled with analogies and anecdotes. I'd take this winding journey with him, unaware of the destination until the very end when he'd reveal how this historic and epic tale of one his past experiences, either in court or otherwise, succinctly and comprehensively answered my question. The guy was a brilliant orator and cunningly persuasive. There's no way that a guy like that could be mistaken for a car salesman, an accountant, or even a doctor. He had lawyer written all over him. Clearly, his worldview was shaped by his profession.

After having spent nearly twenty years of my life as a health-care administrator, having been everything from a research assistant to a regional vice president, I tend to see things from a clinical perspective. The good part about that is that I tend to think systematically and logically, being driven by evidence and data. The bad part is that I think every pain or ailment is some rare form of cancer or congenital heart condition. I'm pretty sure I've been self-diagnosed with at least three different kinds of cancer and one heart condition. Despite my baseless paranoia, recurring headaches are not necessarily brain cancer. Most likely, they're due to seasonal allergies. A Zyrtec would probably be much more effective than chemotherapy. It reminds me of the line in *Kindergarten Cop* that was so perfectly delivered by the former governor of California: "It's not a tumor." No genius, it's not a tumor; it's just gas. Go fart and be cured.

As I reflect on my life and the role that society has played in shaping my development, I can see similarities in American culture and a disease with which I am intimately familiar: cancer. Indulge me for a minute while I set the stage for the rest of the book. This section is a little academic, but like a great movie, you have to set up the background before you get to the action so you know what's going on. At its most fundamental level, cancer is the rapid and uncontrollable multiplication of abnormal cells. Normal, healthy, cells have a life cycle, which maintains a balance of cells in quantity and biological barrier. Essentially, cells are meant to stay in their lane and experience a natural creation and self-destruction process. Cancer cells behave differently. They don't adhere to the normal life cycle, and they don't obey the normal biological barriers that confine them to the designated areas of the body. Cancer may manifest in a variety of ways and in almost every organ. Not only does it originate in a primary area, sort of a ground zero, it has a tendency to spread to other organs or metastasize. This metastatic activity significantly increases the chances for more severe damage to the overall body, even to the point of death.

Like the culture of any country, America has a litany of societal norms and traditions, which flow through the blood of many American citizens. We enjoy fireworks and barbeque on the fourth of July, and leaving cookies for Santa Clause on Christmas Eve hoping to atone for those occasional "naughty" days throughout the year. Those norms and many others give us our identity as a nation and are necessary to provide a sense of belonging and commonality. Within the culture as a whole, there are subcultures that often provide influence in one way or another. Oftentimes, that influence is intentional as in incidences of evangelism or conversely episodes of oppression, while other times, that influence may be unplanned or reactionary as in occasions of benevolence to a stranger. The challenge arises when negative instances of influence fail to have a life cycle and instead perpetuate harmful behaviors that rarely remain localized and often cross-cultural and geographic boundaries. These metastatic behaviors are seen in phenomena like homophobia, racism, sexism, classism, and any other "ism" that leads to someone being discriminated against because of our differences.

The prognosis sounds bleak. Right? Well, here's the good news. There is a treatment that can at least lead to a better quality of life, if not to a cure for what ails our society. As with any disease, the best cure is prevention. Organizations like the American Cancer Society and the National Institutes of Health have invested significant resources in prevention efforts to avoid the onset of preventative diseases. Many times, we create environments for ourselves or place ourselves in environments that can be hazardous. While asbestos exposure may lead to mesothelioma, exposure to racially insensitive communities leads to generations of uneducated men and women that nurture a cycle of hate toward people who differ from them. There are prevention efforts in which we can engage to deter bigotry and hatred.

When prevention fails or when we're past the stage of prevention and symptoms have manifested, we must work to discover the root of the problem through diagnosis. Technology has made medical advancements possible that allow clinicians to view hidden organs in 3D and witness the patterns of microscopic organisms. We can look below the surface to understand the origin of the condition. Based on the anatomical region, different instruments are used to better understand the genesis of the problem. To understand the psychology of a subculture, we must examine different facets of life within that context to appropriately diagnose the condition of a population. Understanding someone's perspective on politics, interpersonal relationships, and economics provides critical information to understand their behavioral patterns. I once heard that you can tell a great deal about a person if you review their bank account. They spend money on their priorities. I would argue that you can find out an equally important amount by checking the names on the ballot they cast, assuming they took advantage of our freedom to vote, and by examining the relationships they maintain and how those relationships are managed.

Lastly, after the problem has been diagnosed, the next step in the process is treatment through one or multiple modalities. Posttreatment, a person's journey takes them in one of two ways. Either the treatment was successful and they need rehabilitation or reintegration through survivorship efforts or the treatment failed and they need to be kept comfortable by means of palliative care while they await their inevitable demise. Treatment for the ills of our society ranges in preference and application. Most often, we tend to treat the symptoms, and not the root cause, through retail therapy, drugs, alcohol, sex, overindulgence in work or hobbies, and anything else that provides a distraction from the true work that we need to do to ameliorate our society. We feel better for a moment, but the symptoms return. We're treating an aneurysm with Advil. It doesn't work, and the danger of continuing this course of treatment leads to certain death. The good news is that it's not too late to change our behavior. We're not a terminal nation but a nation that has demonstrated its ability to be strong and resilient as individual communities. The time has come, however, for us to collectively discuss issues of relevance to redefine our destiny, by developing a treatment plan that aims to identify, diagnose, and destroy the disease rather than just managing the symptoms. Now, it is time for the action.

Harvey Eve

I'd worked for months to pull together two very important meetings. I had successfully organized a group of leaders and physicians that would create an alliance between the two largest subspecialty health-care organizations in Texas. It took a considerable amount of time, energy, and social capital to bring it together. Meanwhile, everyone in the state of Texas was glued to the television as reports of the impending hurricane came more and more frequently. I've lived in Texas all of my life, spending the majority of that time in Houston. I've seen many hurricanes and tropical storms. I wasn't intimidated by Harvey. The initial reports of the trajectory were inconsistent. It's hard to detect the exact path of a hurricane until it's too late to do anything about it. I guess God is tricky that way.

Executives from across the country were flying in for my meetings. The presentations were set, accommodations were made, and I was poised to make a huge contribution to my company, which would propel my career forward by leaps and bounds. On the afternoon of Wednesday, August 23, 2017, I asked my assistant to send an email confirming attendance for the Friday meeting. There was significant enthusiasm from the parties involved, so confirmations began rolling in almost immediately. "Yes, I plan to attend" was the initial response from most. That soon changed, however, as our media outlets continued to blast us with increasingly frightening estimates of Hurricane Harvey's impact. I saw my work unraveling before my eyes. *Fucking Harvey*, I thought as I read email after email that suggested we postpone our meeting. I wasn't alone in that sentiment. One of the other leaders of the organization pressed hard to move forward with the meeting, even suggesting a teleconference. Some meetings are best had face-to-face, so that was quickly shot down by senior leadership.

My Friday meeting was canceled. The mega alignment that I was planning would have to wait. Based on the trajectory of the storm, we learned that Houston was going to be on the "dirty" side, incurring significant negative impacts because of the wind force and speed of the trajectory. The city of Houston was absolutely devastated. This was no fire drill. This was the real thing. Not only was Houston on the dirty side, but while many citizens and celebrities rallied to rescue people from homes and raise money to help rebuild the many crippled communities, Harvey made me see how dirty life can be. Homes were decimated by dirty water, leaving dirty sheet rock and soggy wood cabinets stacked six feet high on street corners. The dirty side of humanity reared its head as looters took advantage of families who evacuated their homes to save their lives but sacrificed their valuables. Rescue boats sliced through dirty water that covered highways and streets normally traveled by passengers in cars, in trucks, on bicycles, and by foot. That dirty water was now home to insects, reptiles, and bacteria of various kinds. Harvey is only a memory now, but remnants of dirty remain.

Thankfully, several brave souls attended the first of my two major meetings. It was Thursday evening, August 24, 2017. It was a major meeting that cast the vision of subspecialized health care in our region. I was responsible for a segment of the care at sixteen hospitals from Conroe to Brownsville. The work that I was doing had never been done before in my company, not in this way and not to this scale. I was endeavoring to pioneer the health care for our region and to do it in a highly competitive atmosphere with health-care leaders peppered across our market. The Thursday meeting went perfectly. The attendees went home that evening motivated and excited about the potential to positively impact the lives of tens of thousands of people. I felt like the Obama of health care. "Yes, we can" change the way health care is delivered for the thousands of patients in the communities we serve. Like our forty-fourth president, I was often the only person in the room with dark skin, trying to influence board rooms full of White men and women. I was thankful, however, that my company possessed strong values and a tremendous ethical code that was engrained into our culture. I was never concerned about racism. I was more concerned about being sharp enough to pull off something that had never been done before because it was always thought to be impossible.

I wound up in a position to influence the care of a region in a fairly circuitous way. After walking into a dark hospital room in June of 1993, interrupting an unknown priest offer a last prayer for my father, I knew I had to do something to impact cancer care. My father died from lymphoma when I was sixteen years old. I watched a strong, fearless man wither away to an almost helpless human being. He went from seemingly superhuman to a mere mortal in a matter of months. His weight diminished drastically, and his hair fell out. His strength was minimized, and his ability to care for himself was severely reduced. Witnessing the rapid deterioration of my father provided the motivation to somehow contribute to cancer research and treatment. After completing my undergraduate degree, I began working for an accounting consulting firm. That couldn't be farther from cancer care, so I decided that I would contribute financially to the American Cancer Society in an effort to fulfill my desire to contribute to fighting the disease. It wasn't enough. I left the consulting gig and went to work in the research department of what has been called, over multiple years, the number one cancer institute in the world. It was an honor to work there. I began my career in cancer care by working with research participants from the local communities who wanted to quit smoking. I was only a research assistant, but I felt like I was making a meaningful impact. Over time, however, that grew to be insufficient as well. I needed to make a larger impact. I spent sixteen years at that institution, assuming various roles and titles, getting promotion after promotion and multiple opportunities to impact care on an increasingly larger scale. For a while, it was fulfilling. But eventually, that wasn't enough. Through life's events, call it the universe, divine guidance, or destiny, I found myself staring at a position that would afford me the opportunity to impact the care of thousands of people in multiple communities across a geography that spanned most of southeast Texas. I became responsible for the cancer care for several diverse populations, perhaps giving me the chance to minimize the number of sons and daughters who walked into dark hospital rooms to interrupt the last prayer of an unknown priest as their loved one slipped into their final rest. I never thought I would have had that role, but like I said before, God is tricky that way.

Limitless Potential

"You can be anything you put your mind to." That was my mom's mantra. She believed that to an extent. She said, "You can even be the president one day if you want." This, of course, was BO (Before Obama). For a while, I actually believed her.

I thought that the sky was the limit for my life. I hadn't been introduced to glass ceilings or crabs in a bucket. I was just a kid with lots of big dreams.

As I got older, the dreams were accompanied by spoilers. I started to see lots of people living my dreams. They had the life I wanted and the nice cars I wanted. In the eighties in South Park, Houston, Texas, the biggest and baddest car was a black Mercedes Benz. It had to be black. That was a statement of power—tinted windows, chrome accents, and shiny rims. What is it about us and rims? We can have a ride that's one spark plug away from the junkyard, but you better believe we *gone have them rims looking fly*. Most of the time, guys in my neighborhood had rims that cost more than the value of the car. They had the big, shiny rims that protruded about ten inches away from the tire. That wasn't exactly my taste. It was cool to look at, but I envisioned them turning into rotating blades with the ability to exact vengeance in road rage on any poor soul that decided to cut them off. The whole *Mad Max* thing wasn't for me. I just liked the factory-style shiny rims. Mercedes Benz options in rims was good enough for me. So I aspired to have the black Mercedes Benz with tinted windows and superfly (factory) rims.

The Black and Brown Burden

Overtime, my mom's language started to change. She went from saying I "can be anything I put my mind to" to "you have to work twice as hard as White people to succeed in this world." In this world? Was there another world I could succeed in where I didn't have to work so hard? Was there an option of going to another world? What kind of passport did I need for that? No, there isn't an alternative universe where race is irrelevant and equality is pervasive. What she meant was that there was no place on this earth where I could go where I wouldn't be impacted by the color of my skin. It was inescapable. I took it as though I had been marked by God and doomed to live a tortured life just because I was born in a certain family with a certain shade of skin color. What did I do to deserve this, God? Why did I have to be born Black?

From my perspective, Black people were relegated to impoverished neighborhoods, menial wages, disadvantaged schools, and perpetual lack. The streets in my neighborhood all had a similar theme. There was a smattering of neatly manicured homes and at least one home that was unexpectedly evacuated yet routinely occupied by opportunistic distributors of select pharmaceuticals (i.e., crack house) and that one house that none of the kids wanted to go to even if their ball landed in the backyard because a crazy old lady in a loose housecoat lived there. Mrs. Jenkins was nasty.

My elementary school was in the middle of inner-city Houston, in a neighborhood called South Park. It was a frequent gathering place for thugs and wannabe gangsters on the weekends. Some Mondays, we'd find forty-ounce bottles of Old English, wrapped in brown paper bags, littered near the monkey bars. I and some of my buddies would "pour out a little liquor" for our homies. We didn't know what that meant at the time. We didn't realize that we were engaging in an act that was meant to memorialize dead friends. We saw it in movies and music videos and thought it was the cool thing to do. That's how lots of kids I grew up with were raised. Hollywood shaped our perspectives.

Similarly, my earliest exposure to White people was what I saw on television. I had an incredibly narrow perspective. Movie stars, politicians, and game show hosts—that was what shaped my view of White America. The tragic reality is that many people around the world have a myopic view of life. We, intentionally or unintentionally, perpetuate harmful and ignorant stereotypes that prohibit meaningful communication and understanding between ethnic groups who differ from us. In a world that is anything but homogeneous, this becomes incredibly life-threatening.

When I was in high school, I joined an organization whose purpose was to prepare young minority men and women for jobs in corporate America through business workshops and summer internships. Ideally, the students in the program would have jobs waiting for them when they finished college. The weekend workshops were typically on the campus of Rice University in Houston, Texas. Students joined the program in summer of their senior year in high school and continued each summer throughout college. It was cool to make friends with Black and Brown people, who had an interest similar to mine. We'd spend all day Saturday together learning about interviewing, business etiquette, learning and managing in the workplace, and the benefits of professional networking. Every summer, we'd take a business trip to some select destination in the United States and spend a full week learning more tools of the trade and sneaking in a little time to hook up with the opposite sex. Yes, we all joined the organization for noble reasons, but anytime you put a group of coeds together and give them hotel rooms in a city far away from home, there will be booty calls.

One Saturday at Rice University, we were wrapping a long day of sessions, and I was walking to my car in the parking lot. The parking lot was not close to the building where we had our workshop, so I had to walk across campus to get there. As I neared my truck, I was approached by two Rice PD officers. They said that there had been an attack on a student in the parking lot and that I needed to come with them. I thought to myself, *What the fuck? Why me?* I'm a fairly compliant guy and was raised to respect police officers and follow the rules, but I was completely confused. They drove me to the police station and put me in an interrogation room. I sat there alone, behind walls of one-way mirrors, to conceal the identity of whomever was on the other side. I have no idea how long I was there, but it seemed like an eternity. I sat there thinking, *Why am I here? What did I do? Why isn't someone coming in here to talk to me?* This was before everyone had cell phones. There was no Snapchat or Facebook Live to stream this. This was just me in a room, waiting for an explanation.

Finally, a police officer comes in and says, "You're free to go. You didn't do it." No shit, I didn't do it. The question is, why was I there? I figured out that they had the victim on the other side of the glass and that I was waiting to be identified. All she had to say was, "Yes, he did it." My life would have changed forever. I was not guilty of any crime. I was coming from a business training session. What I didn't tell you before is that at each weekend session, we were required to wear business casual attire. We were also required to be neatly manicured as if we were going to an off-site business meeting with corporate leadership. I was wearing a button-down long sleeve shirt and khaki pants. My hair was neatly cut, fresh from the barbershop, and I had a neatly trimmed mustache. Why am I describing this to you in such great detail? Because perhaps you're thinking that I looked intimidating or out of place on the campus of a university.

When I tell other people this story, even back then, they said that they couldn't imagine me being stopped and harassed. They know me as kind, thoughtful, ambitious, intelligent, articulate, and not menacing and threatening. My clothes were not at all disheveled, and I had no defensive marks or scratches. What made me a potential suspect? While my business casual attire was appropriate for the setting, the melanin that I wear sometimes attracts the wrong attention. My experiences have taught me that it's not often in style to wear this skin color or this hair texture in certain places in this country. I've learned that my intellect and my socioeconomic status will never outweigh the burden of being Black. For a few gut-wrenching minutes, my fate was in the hands of a random girl on a college campus. Even if I had gone to court and won, this event would have followed me in one way or another for the rest of my life. I was uncomfortably close to becoming a part of the statistics that demonstrate that while African Americans make up approximately 13 percent of the population, we account for 47 percent of 1900 exonerations and a majority of 1800 additional innocent victims who were framed in fifteen large-scale police scandals. We make up a disproportionate amount of the incarcerated and wrongly accused population.

Let's revisit my attire. Remember the khaki pants and button-down shirt I was wearing on the campus of Rice University? In August of 2017, a group of about 250 White nationalists invaded the campus of the University of Virginia the day before the Unite the Rite rally. They were wearing khaki pants and polo shirts. They carried torches, organized in mass two by two, and flooded a university campus with the intent to intimidate and harass. They encircled thirty students of various Color and chanted hateful words, some making monkey noises at the Black students. None of them were arrested. None of them were taken to an interrogation room. None of them were questioned at all for their actions; instead, they were protected by their constitutional right to gather and publicly demonstrate. I'm told that "there were some very fine people on both sides."

CHAPTER 2

Siblings, Sam, and Dr. Frankenstein

In the Beginning

In the beginning, it was all of us in the same room. Well, at least my two brothers and me. My sister had her own room. I love my sister now, but I couldn't stand her when we were all growing up. I'm not sure why. There's an old wives' tale that says that if you make someone angry while they're pregnant that their child will look like you. Perhaps she would look like me anyway considering we share a gene pool, but I made sure to annoy the piss out of her every single day to make sure that she would see my sarcastic face on her little bundle of joy every time she looked at it. To this day, I can't tell you why I didn't like her. I just didn't. She didn't like me either. It was mutual disdain between us.

There's a significant age gap between my siblings and me. I was an accident. I'll admit it. My closest sibling is thirteen years away in age. The next one? Fourteen years away. The other? Fifteen years away. You see a trend here? Clearly, my siblings were purposefully staggered by a year. I, on the other hand, was the product of a determined little sperm cell that fought through a premenopausal canal that had well retired all inclinations of contractions, labor, and delivery years earlier. There's no way that my mom and dad were like, "Hey, you bored? Let's make a baby so we can sleep less, spend more money, and start all over after getting all our kids to high school and damn near out of the house. We have *way* too much time, energy, and money. Let's do it." So essentially, I was raised as an only child. I mean, my sister was there long enough for me to terrorize her just a little, and then she left the house when she got married to her good-for-nothing first husband. I understand that marriages don't always work out. Believe me, I understand that concept, and I'll elaborate on it later, but I give him the big middle finger salute because he elected to deny his daughter a face-to-face meeting, much less any semblance of a relationship. When your daughter reaches out to you when she becomes an adult; chooses to give you a pass on every birthday you missed, every father/daughter event, and every major life event; and extend an invitation to your sorry ass for just a meeting, you accept! This spineless penis wrinkle stood her up instead. I don't care about his issues with my sister. I care about his lack of respect and appreciation for a beautiful girl that he donated sperm for. But I digress. There's a special place in the fifth layer of hell for him.

My sister was actually kind of a big deal in high school. She briefly dated a, now hall of fame, basketball player before he became famous when she was in high school. I'm not sure how she ended up with her fecal-matter first husband. I'm talking about an extreme pendulum swing. She was, and is, pretty although I would never have admitted that to her when I was younger. She was a majorette and was pretty popular. After she rebounded from her first marriage, she married a guy that she'd known for years. It turns out he's a pretty good guy. They've been married for a gajillion and one years and have three girls total.

My middle brother, the guy who's fourteen years older than me, had his own claim to fame in high school as well. He actually left my parents' house when he was a teenager to live with our grandmother in Temple, Texas. It's a small town just outside of Waco (you know a town is small when you use another small town to reference it as the better known, big city). Though he's shortest of us all, he was the most accomplished athlete. He played high school football and has always excelled at strength and power sports. My oldest brother, I'll talk about him in a minute, introduced me to weight lifting, but my middle brother helped me fall in love with it. I went to my first body-building competition with him. It is pretty cool to be in the presence of these massive athletes who have dedicated so much time, energy, and other resources to achieve their physique.

After high school, he made his own path in life. He has three boys, one girl, and a wife whom he seems to adore. They have a nice, blended, family with their own dynamics and complications. They make it work though. I like his wife and their relationship. She's good for him. I think he's able to see life more clearly when he looks through her eyes. Her perspective is challenging, yet refreshing for him. That seems to be what successful relationships do, right? It will challenge you at times but push you to be a better person more often than not. As long as challenging doesn't turn into driving you batshit crazy and as long as pushing you to be a better person feels like some-one standing in your corner cheering your success and encouraging endurance during the times when you're ready to tap out, then I'd say you're on the right track.

My oldest brother was always seen as the wild one. He's the most like my dad. My brother has the ability to demonstrate the charm and charisma necessary to make one feel as though they are the single most important person in the entire world. On the other hand, putting on his badge to go to work seems to work as his mean button that transforms those usual friendly neighborhood red spider man qualities to the black venom spider man that becomes a menace to society. I suppose he has to channel his inner bully to face the evil that lurks in our city, waiting for an opportunity to take a purse, a car, or a life. Fight fire with fire, right? We would probably all do well with a mean button from time to time. Life, at times, favors those who elect to fight instead of take the higher ground. Sometimes, getting in the fight and slinging a little mud is the only thing that people respond to. Mike Tyson once said, "Everyone has a plan until they get punched in the mouth." Sometimes, you need to be able to disrupt the plans of those who seek to harm you by punching them in the mouth, metaphorically speaking. We'll talk more about the power of the "punch" in later chapters.

Meet Sam

There's one more distant relative I should discuss at this point. I've always felt like society, whom I'll affectionately refer to as "Sam" since I grew up knowing America as "Uncle Sam," was inherently at odds with me. Sam does not represent all of society, but the society that embraces philosophies and bolsters institutions and cultural traditions that serve to marginalize and minimize the progress of Black and Brown people. Sam wasn't my uncle or anyone in my family. My family was clearly a darker shade of brown. Sam and I weren't related. We were adversaries. While many were inspired by patriotic rhetoric that lauded the fabled figure who so cleverly resembled Abraham Lincoln, one of the most beloved and historic presidents in the history of our country, I initially feared Sam. The draft was still alive and well when I was growing up. Sam was the guy who took young Black men away from their families to fight for a country that didn't feel like it was fighting for them. Many of my friends were hopeful that the benefits of serving their country would lead them to a better life and would secure a safe and successful future for them and their families. The problem with that was that it wasn't guaranteed. Many of the young brave men in the generation before me returned home with addictions that they developed while serving to cope with the stress they endured. It happens, I guess. People do what they have to do to cope. They also returned from duty to be met with a lack of opportunity for good jobs. They were told that they didn't have experience or transferable skills. That's tough to risk your life to save others who would never know you and return to the denial of opportunities from those same people you fought to defend. I admit that I'm a bit cynical. I'm incredibly grateful for my country and for the soldiers who fought and continue to fight to defend it. However, my perspective needed time to evolve. I needed to examine our incredibly diverse country from numerous angles to get a more comprehensive picture of the complexity of the inequities that exist. I needed to take a closer look at our society and a closer look at my own prejudices to understand what was influencing my views.

Creating a Role Model

Needless to say, I didn't feel like I fit in anywhere as a kid. I felt like I was a foreigner living in a country that didn't reflect me or accept me. I was a very quiet kid. Part of it had to do with my speech impediment, and the other was just due to my personality. I was an extreme introvert. To some extent, I still am. However, I've learned to manage my stutter significantly better as an adult. Gone are the days of gggetting st...st...stuck on words in every sentence I speak. It was mortifying. Imagine being chubby, having a face full of acne, and incomprehensible because I would get caught in fits of face-contorting, spit-slinging stuttering. Now that's a guy you want to bring home to Mama, right? Needless to say, I kept my mouth shut as much as possible. I once thought I could quit stuttering by imitating other people. I tried doing impressions of various movie stars, and that actually seemed to work. The problem was that I sounded like an idiot. No one wanted to hear a little Black kid from cloverland talk like Sylvester Stallone. Again, it really sounds like a winner that the family should meet, right? #epicfail

As I matured, however, I figured out how to solve problems and overcome adversities like stuttering. I refused to allow mainstream society to oppress me for the rest of my life. It had already created a world that judged me according to the color of skin instead of according to the words that would flow, or not flow, from my mouth and the content of my character. My methodology is a bit unconventional but effective. For some reason, I've always had an intimate relationship with anger. I remember coming home after school and working on my homework in my bedroom. I'd get so frustrated with my math homework. I'd sit there staring at the page as if the math gods were, at any moment, going to cause the answers to leap from the text into my brain. That never happened. What did happen was that the longer I stared at the page, the more I boiled with anger like a cast iron pot on an old gas stove. I'd get to a point where my anger boiled over, and I'd throw the book across the room, hurling profanities under my breath so my parents couldn't hear, whisper-yelling something that I'd never even think to say at an audible level. You know when you try to yell while you're whispering so you get the intensity of a yell but the volume of a whisper? I'd be like, "St…st… stupid ass math. Who needs this shit? Fuck algebra, fuck my algebra teacher, and f-f-fuck my st…st…stupid ass school for making me take this w-w-wack ass s-s-subject. All anybody really needs is addition. I can add! Two plus two equals four, bitch! Letters sh…sh… shouldn't even be in m-m-motherfucking math, no way!"

Then after my flurry of fucks and other random expletives, I'd settle down and take a breath, and voila, the answer would arrive. It became as clear as crystal. So as unorthodox as this may seem, I adopted it as my problem-solving strategy—anger. Who would have thought it could be such an agent of progress?

These days, anger primarily fuels my various workout styles and, to some extent, continues to work as a problem-solver. I still get angry when I can't figure something out. I still whisper-yell curse words, sometimes at home just out of range of the kids hearing and sometimes at work in my office. It still proves to be effective although I've tried to adopt meditation as a more socially acceptable and peaceful solution. But anger still has its place. It's like that secret little indulgence that you keep buried away 90 percent of the time, only allowing it to surface temporarily for special occasions.

I've evolved from fuck algebra to fuck Sam. Sam will not dictate my success, my happiness, my prosperity, and my place in the world. Sam will not overlook me and give to others that which I rightfully deserve. Sam will be forced to recognize me because I'm going to punch him in the mouth to keep disrupting his plans for me. I will not be mediocre. I will be brilliant.

Anger propelled me to create a role model. I knew I needed to look toward something bigger than me and something more tangible than religion. I needed to find someone who had done what I wanted to do so I could emulate them. I never found that person. What I found was "those people." My role model was not one Black knight in shining armor sent to pave a path of glory to show me the way. My role model was a compilation of three prominent Black men when I was growing up. I wanted to be influential and to be well-spoken, and I wanted to, one day, leave my mark on the world for doing something that changed the way people think about a relevant issue. I wanted to raise Sam's social consciousness in a way that challenged people's long-standing views and forced them to reevaluate their position. Even though this guy was dead by the time I was forming my own opinions and was highly flawed as most of us are, Dr. Martin Luther King Jr. served as one of my role models. Watching clips of his speeches and understanding the impact that he had on people of all races were electrifying. He could galvanize masses of people. He could deliver speeches with grace and elegance enough to propel action. He was a leader of many and a role model to even more. This guy touched a nation and did so without the luxury of wealthy and well-connected family members. He was just a Black kid from Georgia with a dream. He did more in his thirty-nine years of life than many people will ever even dream of doing. Granted, we know that he was a mere mortal and wrestled with demons and various vices, but that doesn't take away from the legacy of his iconic life. I chose to focus on Dr. King, the public figure and civil rights rap god. That was the cool thing about creating a role model. I could be Dr. Frankenstein; take parts from this person, parts from that person; and create the model that fit me and my goals.

My next role model was Billy D. Williams. Martin had elegance and influence, but Billy D had swag. When I was growing up, Billy D was the guy that women admired and guys wanted to be. He was acting in movies, television, commercials, and everything. I've always wanted to have charisma that translated on both the large scale, talking to crowds of thousands, and the small scale, talking one-on-one with someone watching them hang on my every word. The guy was magnetic. He was the most interesting man in the world before the most interesting man in the world. In his day, he was the personification of sophistication, masculinity, and self-awareness. He understood his brand and knew the value of his brand—his personal brand. He knew who he was and leveraged that persona to his benefit. Entertainers after him like Prince shared that characteristic. They weren't interested in fitting in. They were interested in being the mold that others would aspire to but never be able to fit in. As one of my best friends likes to say it, they were "comfortable in their own skin." That's what I wanted.

My last role model has recently fallen from grace like a man jumping out of an airplane without a parachute. I'm saddened to know that the man who represented one of my childhood heroes was engaged in illegal activities that victimized women and took advantage of them in their most vulnerable state. I personally stand in solidarity with the women and vehemently denounce his actions. Despite his own personal demons, during his era, there was no greater picture of a Black father than "Heathcliff Huxtable" portrayed by Bill Cosby. *The Cosby Show* itself was a monumental leap for not only Black people but for the entire viewing population. It was the first time in mainstream media that Hollywood saw the power of positive images of Black people. We could finally be seen as more than drug dealers, gangbangers, and wayward men in local productions of *Chitlin' Circuit* plays.

I appreciate the images of Nino Brown from *New Jack City* that made its way to the big screen. One of my favorite movie quotes of all time was delivered by Wesley Snipes in that movie: "Sit your five-dollar ass down before I make change." I loved it. But the Black experience demonstrated through the visual arts became myopic. We are as multifaceted as the next culture. There is good, bad, and ugly in Black people just as in any other. So why not show it? Because Hollywood didn't think that the general viewing public would believe it. If they don't believe it, they don't watch it. If they don't watch it, they don't make money. After all, who would believe that a Black male doctor would marry a Black female lawyer and raise four semi-well-adjusted kids and have problems that could be relatable to a broad base of viewers? Millions believed, and so did I. I wanted to be a Heathcliff Huxtable dad. My father and I didn't have the greatest relationship. As I mentioned, he died shortly before I graduated high school, and for the majority of my life, I hated him. He was mean. He was absent for the majority of my life. He would get drunk. He would step out on my mom over the years. There was one time he came home drunk and found me in bed with my mom. He was pissed. He wanted me to go back to my bed and go to sleep. I couldn't. There was a huge rat underneath my bed that found its shelter there for whatever reason. Some way, I heard it squeaking, and I decided to spend the night with my mom.

When my dad got home, he made me crawl under the bed, grab the rat with a newspaper as a barrier, and squeeze it until it died. I was petrified. I stayed there staring at the rat eye to eye for what seemed like hours. My father stood behind me yelling, "Pick up the got damn rat!" For some reason, the rat didn't move either. It just stood there. I don't know if it was sick, dying, or just as petrified as I was. There was a large field behind my childhood home, so perhaps it found its way in from there. After a while, my father grew impatient. He made a fist with his large, blue-collar hands and punched me in the back of the head.

"Pick up the rat!"

Again, he punched me. Finally, as my eyes filled with water and my hands shook, I grabbed the rat with the newspaper.

"Now, pick it up and squeeze it! And you better not start crying!"

My dad could see my eyes welling up. He didn't believe in crying, not for boys. He wasn't "raising no sissy." So I did what he said. My mom watched in horror, pleading with my dad to stop. He ignored her. I took the rat outside and threw it in the trash—newspaper and all. I wasn't sure if the rat were dead or not, so I sprayed bug spray in its face while it lay motionless on top of a pile of trash in the trash can. That image is just as vivid today as it was when it happened. I can still feel water begin to collect in my eyes as I remember that event, but not a tear will drop. I ascribe to the philosophy that you can learn something from everyone, so I know that I learned hard work from my dad. I learned that if you want something, you have to work your ass off to get it. There's no way around it. So in a way, he contributed to Dr. Frankenstein's creation.

He tried to teach me a trade, I guess. He knew how to work on anything that had an engine. He went from being a shade tree mechanic to becoming an automated valve specialist. He understood the fundamental principles of mechanics, so he could apply that to any engine. In a way, I guess those nights when he'd work on cars in our driveway, he expected me to take an interest like my oldest brother. That was never my thing though. I'd watch for a little bit, but then I'd get bored. Working underneath a car, getting motor oil all over you while swatting at ghetto-squitos, was never appealing to me, especially not when I had an Atari in the house just waiting to be played. Do you know how fun it was to play pong? Don't even get me started on Galaga. That was my jam! Besides, who wants to come in the house after being outside for three hours at night with fifty-two mosquito bites? Apparently, our mosquitos had a mutation that made them replicate when you slapped them. They were like *Bebe's Kids*. They didn't die. They multiplied. So I decided at a young age that I'd rather make enough money and pay someone who learned the trade to do the work for me instead of learning the trade myself. I guess that could be perceived as arrogant, but I needed my own motivation to reach my potential. If avoiding the attack of the "ghetto-squitos" motivated me to study harder in school at the hope of getting a good enough job to pay someone to fix my car, then so be it.

Dr. Huxtable was the sensible, intelligent, fun-loving, supportive dad who demonstrated the ability to succeed regardless of your starting point in life. He made me realize what a Black family could be. We can be happy. We can be encouraging. We can make family skits and lip-sync songs to entertain everyone at important family occasions. We could be rich! What? Yes, rich. We can be powerful, successful contributors in Sam's America and not be an athlete, entertainer, or drug dealer. Nothing against professional athletes or entertainers, I wish I had their skill, but I don't. Most people don't. We needed another alternative. We needed to know that we have more options to succeed. The Cosbys gave us that option, and Heathcliff Huxtable gave me the dad that I wished I had.

God Help Me Make It Through High School

Church Life

I remember faking like I was sick on Sunday mornings. I hated going to church. It was incredibly boring. They didn't have all these cool youth groups and youth church options like they do now, at least not in my neighborhood. They tried that for a little while. It sucked. It consisted of kids being stowed away in temporary buildings behind the main sanctuary, learning various derivations of biblical stories. They tried to make it hip, but it just made me question the authenticity. Pontius Pilate wasn't "straight up trippin' when he sent 5-0 to bust a cap in Jesus." I hadn't read the Bible at that time, but I was pretty sure it didn't happen like that.

I went back to sit in the big people church with my mom and all the other paper fan-waving, clock-watching, half-gossiping, half-singing adults. It took me forever to learn the words *at the cross* because the people around me kept changing the words. For the longest time, I thought it was, "At the cross, at the cross, girl, can you believe that dress? Sister Johnson knows she is wrong for looking a hot me...yeeess."

Over time, I learned to appreciate church. I actually fell in love with it. The idea of enjoying a community of people who believed what I believed and who tried to live according to the same standards was appealing to me. The idea of church and Christianity was always beautiful to me. In theory, it worked well. It even held up in many real-life situations for me. I relied on my relationship with God, specifically Jesus Christ, so heavily as a kid more so than you would expect from someone my age at the time. I had a sort of blind faith, believing that the words in a mythical and sacred book were true down to the punctuation. I'll never forget sitting in church when I was in high school, and I thought, *What if my intellect someday outweighs my faith?* Even though I was a strong believer, or so I believed, I needed proof. I've always thought that there must be a way to reconcile the historical events that took place in the Bible with factual, and historical, evidence. I longed for proof, not to solidify my faith but to use as ammunition to all the nonbelievers, the atheists, the Muslims, the Jews, the Buddhists, the Hindus, and the non-Christians. I wanted to prove them wrong. I wanted to finally say, "Ha! My God is the real God. I'm right. You're wrong." So I started learning about Christian apologetics. Admittedly, I've only scratched the surface in what that has to offer, but it seemingly argues more for the existence of a god instead of for the Christian God. Sure, science can't explain many natural phenomena. I got it. But can the existence of the Christian God and only the Christian God be the answer? To be honest, I'm still searching for that answer. The story is even more complicated when you examine the origin of the Abrahamic religions, you know, those other "wrong" religious groups Jews and Muslims. The genesis of the three is interwoven. The gumbo becomes even thicker when you discover that ancient Egyptian religions that predate Christianity talk about the Son of God who came to earth in human form and who was persecuted, died, and raised to life again. It sounds familiar, right? Don't get me wrong. I'm still a Christian, and I still believe in Jesus Christ. My perspective is wider, however. My acceptance of possibilities is greater, and my exploration is deeper. I've adopted more Buddhist practices lately because that resonates with me. Meditating and focusing on minimizing suffering for myself and others make sense to me. It's not too churchy, and there's no fire and brimstone attached.

But as a child, it was all Jesus all the time. Every Sunday, we'd go to church and listen to a half-hour lecture about how we needed to give to the building fund. Every Black church I've ever visited has had a building fund. Seriously, can we not figure out legitimate financing and find a construction company to actually get it done? I've seen churches have building funds for twenty years and never lay a brick on the ground.

My religious foundation has played a significant role in the man I've become. I'd like to believe that I'm a highly principled, though highly flawed, man because of my belief system. I waited until I was in my twenties to have sex. I tried to wait until I was married. Hey, E for effort, right? Hopefully, God grades on a curve. I have a horrible time lying and feel incredible guilt when I do so. It just doesn't sit right with me. I have a very generous heart, sometimes to a fault. I mean seriously, growing up, I was all about the ten commandments. Now, I've broken several of them, several times, since then. I'm not proud of it, but I admit it. The challenging thing for me and Christianity has always been the battle of guilt versus grace. God offers grace, and man doesn't. We're commanded to forgive others as we have been forgiven, but that doesn't happen often. Grace toward ourselves or to our fellow man has never been a strong point for humans, Christians included.

I've hurt many people in my life. Though it was never intentional, it happened. The struggle to extend grace to myself has been so difficult because of the messages that I received growing up. "The wage of sin is death." The prominent message I heard was that of punitive justice, not loving grace. Grace was reserved for those people in the Bible we read about that went on to do great things. The prostitute who washed Jesus's feet with her hair, the adulterer who had his mistress's husband killed, and the murderer who killed Christians for fun, all of those people are critical figures in the Christian story and were horribly flawed, but we read stories about them with such reverence and respect, yet we look at each other and ourselves as if we're worthless. But to be a Black family in Bible Belt America, you were expected to go to church, a Black church. It is the kind of church that lasted for four hours and had that one old lady in her unofficially reserved seat on the third pew, who always seemed to "catch the spirit" every Sunday toward the end of the sermon. I swear if I had a dollar for every time Sister Wilkerson fell out, hat going one way, shoes going another, and started speaking in tongues, I'd be rich. Astonishingly, she'd be okay as soon as the pastor said "amen." I visited a Pentecostal church that took it to a whole new level. They had a practice of running around the sanctuary when they felt the spirit. If they really felt it, they'd make it rain for the pastor, throwing dollars at the pulpit on their second or third lap. I'm all for a deep communing with God and experiencing an intimate and impactful relationship, but I'm not sure if cardio is considered an offering in biblical standards. Burpees for Jesus!

Looking beyond the antics and my cynicism, the Black church experience and developing a relationship with God were deeply impactful and shaped the course of my life and the perspectives I hold. Later in life, I ventured to non-Black churches. That evolved my perspective even more. The greatest difference I saw was that Black churches tended to highlight a longing to overcome current suffering.

"When your light bill is due, call Jesus. When you lose your job, call Jesus."

In, let's call them White churches. The dialogue was different. It was more about "look at how great God is." "What can we do for the less fortunate?" "Isn't God just mighty and wonderful?" It's amazing how one can go from a God who rescues you in need to a God who is admonished because of a life of abundance. Even in church, the experience is different for young Black kids, growing up in historically Black churches. I was surrounded by my blackness. Religion was no relief from the problems I faced, nor was it a beacon of hope for better. It was beacon for baseline. Just getting out of the hole seemed to be the focus. What about living the life of those people in the church across the tracks? I could never accept the philosophy of things getting better when I got to heaven. What about now? If others can live in abundance now, then why can't I? There were so many elements of religion that I've had to wrestle with and seek to reconcile over the years. While I reconcile, I've decided to focus my efforts on augmenting my spirituality. I prefer to strip the man-made dogma for now and focus on connecting with God through nature, through spending quality time with loved ones, through giving to those in need, and through meditation. Right now, that's more important to me than a perpetual building fund.

High School Basketball

One of the hazards of growing up in the hood is that you get teachers and coaches that may or may not be qualified to coach anywhere else. They may be well qualified, but that doesn't mean they should be influencing young minds in any impactful way. In high school, I had two basketball coaches I'll never forget. I won't even get started on "Coach Bear." That dude was one of the scariest men I ever saw. I don't know if *Bear* was his given name or a nickname, but he very much fit the description—tall, wide, hairy, and limited communication skills. I wasn't overly excited about joining a football team that was known more for the band's half-time show than athletic prowess, but Coach Bear definitely squelched any dreams I had of trying out for the team. Besides, I played football in middle school, and all I got out of that experience was a broken thumb and memories of being forcibly thrown out of the boys' locker room, into a gym where a million other students were, in nothing but my jockstrap. I decided to pass on the pigskin.

Basketball, on the other hand, was calling my name. If I had to highlight two pillars that were indicative to the Black experience, I'd have to say church and basketball. Those two activities seemed to be universal pastimes for Black people around the country. I thought I had a shot at a letterman's jacket. Letterman's jackets led to popularity, and popularity led to girls. That's what it's all about in high school, right? Validation and girls. I'll never forget there was a girl that I had a huge crush on. She was athletic and smart, had beautiful skin and pretty eyes, and had a big ass boyfriend that played football and who was as dumb as a box of rocks. That cat couldn't spell football. We were between classes one day, and I caught up to her for a quick chat. I'm throwing my best game, which was horrible, feeling like I had her hanging from my every word. I notice her turn her head a little bit, and I thought she was either confused or really just digging what I was saying so much that it was as if she was saying, "Awwww, he's so sweet." All of a sudden, in a tone that was all too audible to the other students around us, she said, "You got a bugger in your nose!" Really? That's your response to all I was saying? All I could do was turn around, walk away, and try to cover my nose as cool as I could. There's really no way to dig a bugger on the sly.

My basketball coaches had to have PTSD. I don't know if it was from the war or the hood, but they had serious issues. One coach liked to pull his players by the shirt when they did something wrong. I came home with a ripped T-shirt almost every night.

"Get down the court, Blackmon! Get in his face, Blackmon! Don't shoot the ball in the other team's goal, Blackmon!"

Typically, the shirt grab was proceeded by, "Get your ass over here!" *Rip.* It wasn't just me. Many of the players had ripped shirts. One time, he pulled my shirt, and it didn't rip. I thought to myself, *Yes, my shirt is still intact.* I swear he read my mind because he called me back over to him just to rip my shirt. I couldn't stand him.

My other basketball coach would never let anyone sit or stand behind him. He seriously flipped out, seriously. Dude was like, "Hey, boy! Don't stand behind me. I don't know what you're doing back there. Don't make me get my knife out!" Only coaches in the hood carry knives to basketball practice. He was probably smart to do so. The kids in my school were crazy. We were segregated by academic program. There were the regular students, the pre-IB students, and the vanguard students. The vanguard kids were supposedly the smart ones. We all had our separate classes, separate hallways, and separate activities. I'll go into more detail about that later, but one of the few things that united us was athletics. The administration of the school facilitated animosity between us. I'm not sure if it was intentional or not, but it happened. The last thing a historically Black high school, in the middle of an all-Black neighborhood, needed was more separation and more stigmas of inferiority. So athletics and student council were for integration. The vanguard kids were mostly scared of the regular kids. Unfortunately, it was akin to Field Negroes versus House Negroes. The jealousy was there. The feelings of inferiority were there. The desire to remain as separate as possible was there.

Back in the day, those jean shorts with thigh-sized leather patches on the front were popular. One day, a girl decided to call another girl's leather patch jean shorts "pleather" or fake leather. The girl wearing the shorts stabbed her. She died. At high school, over shorts, they were "regular" students. It was unfortunate that they furthered the stereotype. Or was it a self-fulfilling prophecy? Do we behave as we believe we ought to based on self-worth interpreted through society's view? I'm not suggesting that we have no responsibility for our actions, but I wonder if we'd value ourselves more, and our stuff less, if we felt like who we are as people is worth more than anything we could ever buy. If I love who I am, then it doesn't matter what you think of me or my shorts.

At basketball practice, we used to "run horses." It was a drill where you divided the basketball court in about six pieces. It was a race, a sadistic race designed by devil-worshipping Nazis, who had nothing better to do than dream up ways to torture overweight Black kids who thought they could play basketball. In order to run horses, you had to run one-sixth of the way, touch the ground, then run back to the start, and touch the ground. Then immediately run one-third of the way, touch the ground, then back to the start, and touch the ground. Then immediately run one-half of the way, touch the ground, then back to the start, and touch the ground. And you'd continue in this fashion until you ran the full length of the court without stopping. It was one of the most tiring exercises we did. Our evil ass coaches would leave it for the very end of practice. For some reason, I feel like I've been running horses for most of my life. I start off strong in a certain direction and then end up back at the start either by my own fear or by missed opportunities. I've never quite been able to get to the end of the court.

For me, high school was the era of *House Party*. Kid 'n Play were hot, high-top fades were the style in the hood, and everybody wanted to dance like Kid 'n Play and throw house parties while their parents were away. I remember I saw *House Party* with my best friend at the time. My mom dropped us off at Gulfgate Mall. The movie theater no longer exists because there were too many occurrences of violence. Apparently, violence off-screen isn't great for ticket sales. It was a cool setup. The movie theater and the mall were separated by a major highway. There was a bridge that connected the two. People used to like hanging out on the bridge to watch the cars speed by beneath. Gangbangers used the mall as their personal canvas, tagging different stores to represent their set. Over the years, the mall has been renovated, and the theater was demolished. Now, all that stands is a bridge to nowhere.

Interestingly, the day I saw *House Party* was the day before Robin Harris, one of the principal actors in the movie, died. That was a surreal moment for me. Robin Harris was one of the Black comedic greats that popularized the badass children that everyone loved to compare their kids to—*Bebe's Kids*. "Bebe's kids don't die. They multiply." From that point on, every unruly Black kid was known as one of Bebe's kids. Kid won't stop talking? Bebe's kid. Kid jumps off the furniture in front of company, wearing nothing but a diaper and a smile? Bebe's kid. Kid slips copious amounts of candy in his diaper at the grocery store while you're standing at the checkout counter arguing over semantics on a coupon for a giant-sized pack of Kool-Aid? Bebe's kid for sure.

CHAPTER 4

Hazed and Confused

One Hundred Thousand by Thirty

When I was a teenager, growing up in southeast Houston (a.k.a. South Park/Sunnyside/Crestmont Park area), I had dreams of making $100K by the time I turned thirty. Looking back on that goal, there were two glaring problems with it: (1) I was aiming way too low. (2) I had no plan of how I'd achieve that goal. Sure, I had thoughts of what I wanted to do when I grew up, but I didn't have a plan. My thoughts were that perhaps I'd be an architect, engineer, or a "businessman." WTF is a "businessman"? My initial major at UT was electrical engineering. I still have scars from the ass whooping I took trying to go through that program. It was clearly not in the cards for me to be a graduate from the UT School of Engineering. I remember spending many nights in the computer labs next to long-bearded skinny White guys who smelled like a puree of Fritos and foot funk. I don't know which was worse, hippie guy who chose not to include hygiene in his daily algorithm or the Asian kid in my class who always finished the assignment so quickly that he chose to play video games in front of everyone else struggling to figure out step one. Fucker, he's either a millionaire with a hot wife and two kids living in Silicon Valley or an overweight consumer of hot pockets, online virtual reality games, and pornography. Just saying, he was headed in one of those directions.

I ended up changing my major several times and dropping classes several times, but I didn't want to. I didn't want to give up. I didn't want it to beat me. I don't think I ever had a true academic challenge before I got to UT. I graduated in the top 5 percent of my high school class. I went to vanguard schools in middle and high school. I thought I was a smart kid. There was also the pressure of the internship I had with, then-named, Houston Lighting and Power. I loved my internship. I'll never forget my boss there. He was a great guy and my first taste at having a mentor. He was a middle-aged White guy who loved working out and bodybuilding. That was right up my alley at that time. We'd leave work sometimes and go work out in the middle of the day. He taught me about drafting in various kinds of software and translating those plans to reality by going in the field and communicating the plans to the linemen. I realize now that the true lesson I learned was to successfully navigate between two worlds and be the liaison between the two to achieve a common goal. There's a soft skill there that is severely underrated.

I remember having a cubicle in an office building in downtown Houston. All the engineers had nice offices with windows. I'd come to work in business casual attire, usually consisting of khaki pants, white shirt, and a tie, complemented by a pair of Cole Haan loafers. I loved shoes growing up. I was raised mostly by my mom and my sister after all. I remember the feeling of importance I had and the feeling of promise I experienced by going into that big, beautiful building every day. I had thoughts of having my own office one day and even being the boss and mentor of other engineers. Another major part of the job was to work with guys who worked to install and replace the equipment in the electrical substations. They were the polar opposite of the white-collar men and women I saw downtown. Their skin had been scorched by the sun, and the wrinkles around their eyes were etched into their skin from perpetual squinting on days they lost, broke, or forgot their shades. Their language wasn't as guarded as the politically correct downtown dwellers, they were free to let the four-letter word fly, and they flung them with great creativity and southern drawl. I liked those guys. They usually looked down on the downtown guys. It was the divide between the "know-it-all" downtown and the guys who did the "real work" in the field. My boss made sure I knew how to walk the walk and talk the talk in both worlds. He didn't want my effectiveness to be stifled by an inability to transform when I needed to.

This is a lesson that would impact the rest of my life. I knew how to adjust my perspective, my language, my walk, my image, and my entire personae when I needed to in order to fit in with my surroundings. I was a chameleon. This was how I navigated life. Around corporate and academic colleagues, I was the articulate, well-read African American who "spoke so well" and seemed "different from what they expected." In the hood, I was the cool homey that stayed to himself and rocked Girbaud jeans with Timberland boots and a FUBU shirt. I remember hearing people say that one must stay true to himself at all times. I didn't really understand that statement until many years later. I thought just the opposite growing up. I thought the only way to get ahead was to become whoever I needed to be in that moment. Whatever that person was expecting was who I became. I struggled with my identity for years because my identity was ever changing and defined by my environment. If I had the opportunity to do it again, I would have spent more time figuring out who I was and less time figuring out who others wanted me to be.

I learned a lot from my time at HL&P. Nevertheless, I changed majors and abandoned that internship. I never saw that boss again. Eventually, I landed on psychology. My major changed, my plans changed, but my goal of making $100K by thirty remained.

I missed my goal. Thirty came and went, and I had not yet made a salary of $100K. It came before I turned forty, but it was a struggle and definitely anticlimactic. I quickly found out that $100K didn't carry the buying power that I expected. I was far from rich, and I made just enough money for Uncle Sam to take more of my money so that $100K didn't feel like $100K. I was working for my employer and working for the government. I wasn't the primary beneficiary of my efforts.

I learned that it wasn't about the money. it was about what I thought it symbolized. I thought $100K would give me success, freedom, a sense of accomplishment, and something to be proud of. I thought I'd be able to buy anything I wanted. I didn't think I'd be rich, but I thought I'd be able to have a nice car, a nice house, nice clothes, and nice anything I could think of. I thought it would be so cool to go to work in a suit and tie every day. Then I did it. And it wasn't what I thought it would be. My professional desires changed over the years. I went from wanting to wear a suit and tie every day and thinking that was success to evolving to believing that the successful ones are the people that can wear whatever the hell they want because they own the business that the suits come to every day. I never knew how to get to that point, however. I didn't have an elaborate, step-by-step plan, and I didn't have a mentor to guide me to success. I didn't even have a picture of someone who was able to accomplish that. I knew doctors and lawyers made a lot of money, but I didn't know anyone personally who had those jobs. I didn't have anyone to talk to so that I could ask questions about the options and the process and the pros and cons of the job. Having that personal touch point can be so incredibly impactful in a person's life.

I remember talking to my best friend in high school, who shares the same name as my son, and we'd swap stories about summer vacation. He'd travel to places around the country with his family, seeing different historical sights and being able to experience the landmarks that we learned about in school. He went to places that I only read about in books. He had family members who had accomplished a number of roles, jobs, etc., and he had friends of family members who he could expand his network to as well. Bryce, my friend not my son, was one of the few White guys at a predominantly Black high school in Houston, but he never let color impact his relationships. Even when Black guys at school would give him a hard time about something, he'd beat them in basketball or at least put up a good game, and they'd give him respect from that point forward. He was also our class valedictorian. He ended up going to West Point and Harvard and now practices law. I haven't talked to Bryce, my friend not my son, in years, but I still relish our high school friendship.

I also appreciate the fact that our relationship, as I examine it retrospectively, taught me about the value of my environment. I grew up surrounded by limitations and a narrow network of people who were also surrounded by limitations. I grew up being told by my mom that I could be anything I wanted to be, but society was telling me through various messages that I had limited opportunities. Statistics has never been in my favor. I remember realizing that as a Black kid in America that it was more likely that I'd end up in jail than end up a doctor. I never did anything that would land me in jail, but my anxiety about being wrongfully accused and sent to prison remained. I also remember thinking that I wasn't sure if I'd make it to the age of twenty-one. I knew guys in my neighborhood and at my high school who didn't. This was my exposure. This was my reality. These aren't excuses for my station in life. They are revelations of elements that make a difference in someone's life as they progress. My goal is to be a light for those around me, even if I come in contact with them for just a short amount of time, to connect them to someone who can help guide their experiences in life. We are only as strong as our network.

Fraternity Life

It's weird how the death of certain men, some famous and some not, have impacted me—Robin Harris, Sammy Davis Jr., my dad, and a guy who used to deal drugs in my neighborhood but who was always cool with me and encouraged me to stay in school. I honestly forgot his name, but let's call him Troy. Troy, Sammy Davis, and my dad all died around the same time. Their deaths hit me like a ton of bricks. For some reason, the death of all those people at once was too much for me to handle at sixteen years old. I knew my dad was going to die, but I didn't. No one told me how sick my dad was, and I always thought he was invincible, so I didn't expect cancer to win. I thought he could fight anything. I knew my dad was going to die because I had a dream that was as clear as a high-definition television where I saw myself delivering a speech where I said, "My dad died when I was sixteen years old." I was fifteen when I had that dream.

I believe that, in some way, the deaths of these "influential men" is related to my desire to be connected with other guys. That sense of brotherhood is appealing to me. Perhaps that's an integral part of my network structure. My natural-born brothers were so much older than me that I didn't develop a strong brotherly relationship with them. We're closer now, but it took thirty years for us to get here. In high school, I joined a high school fraternity. I thought I had found a group of guys that I could form a bond with that would endure for all eternity. I thought I found my ticket to becoming popular and ending my postpubescent awkwardness—not exactly. I was still awkward, and there were only a handful of guys I could relate to in the group. I enjoyed a little popularity, and it was fun to belong to something larger than myself, but I still felt alone. I felt like the world was moving around me, my high school frat included, and I was having an outer-body experience as I passively watched on the sideline.

I remember watching *A Different World* when I was growing up, thinking how cool it would be to attend a Historically Black College or University (HBCU) and joining a frat. The romanticized scenes of compassionate dorm directors, who facilitated the transition of living away from home for the first time, completely resonated with me. I looked forward to the day that I had that one professor who was only tough because he wanted the best of his students and aspired for them to be the best versions of themselves despite battling prejudice and societal marginalization. It helped, of course, that this was a spin-off to *The Cosby Show* as well. Cliff Huxtable and his daughter, Denise, attended the imaginary but prestigious Hillman University. It was a school steeped in history that nurtured and developed the aspirations of young Black students from around the country. If there were ever anything that cemented my desire to go to college, it was this show. I'd always been told by my mom, and believed, that I'd go to college, but it certainly wasn't the experience in my neighborhood. In my small circle, two of my three childhood neighborhood friends attended and graduated from college. One of those colleges was barely a college. Let me rephrase that. The level of academics varies by major, as in most universities, but the school was definitely challenged to recruit academically gifted students as evidenced by the minimal admission criteria. The school was plagued by a grossly disorganized administrative staff. Admission applications were frequently lost. Communication to students regarding transfer documentation and transcripts was abysmal. A potentially good school was self-sabotaged by poor management. Unfortunately, this school was a frequent destination for Black students and run by Black administration. We have to do better for our people in order for our people to do better.

My other friend went to a different local university and became an optometrist. I didn't even know what that was back in the day. Was it a doctor? Was it a guy that sold eyeglasses? I wasn't sure. All I figured was that he was the smartest, and most mature, of all of us and would be rich someday. Who knows? Perhaps he is. I haven't talked to him since he went to college. We played basketball together in my third friend's backyard. My third friend, let's call him "D," had a backyard that was the setting for many of our Saturday adventures. We used to play basketball from the time the sun came up until the streetlights came on. Most of the time, we'd press our luck and play past the streetlight deadline. My mom would step outside the front door and yell, "Baaaarreeeetti" D's house wasn't far away. At one point in time, all of our moms or grandmothers did that. That's just how it was in my neighborhood.

Most of the time, it was the three of us playing, but occasionally, another guy would come over to play. Let's call that guy "J." J was the neighborhood drug dealer, but he was cool. J was a good guy, he just felt like he needed a hustle. I never knew much about J's family situation, but I knew he sold some variety of drugs, mostly weed, but I stayed away from that side of him, so I don't know much about it. Actually, J encouraged us all to stay away from drugs. He never tried to sell to us. He never even offered to us. He knew that we were "good kids" and trying to do well in school to make something of our lives. I actually visited my old neighborhood a few years ago and saw J. He rolled through in a late model sedan with dark shades on and a smile a mile wide across his face. He was happy to see me. I think he was happy to see that I grew up as he thought I would, a stable, straitlaced professional with some kind of office job.

My life's path didn't lead me to an HBCU as I thought. Instead, I ended up getting a scholarship to the University of Texas at Austin. I loved my college years, and I think UT is one of the best schools in the nation, but Austin and my time at UT certainly gave me an awakening to the racism that still exists in our nation and in the fabric of various communities. I was standing in front of Jester during a popular track and field event called Texas Relays. Thousands of people populated Austin to participate in the athletic games, the partying and debauchery, or both. Cars drove up and down the strip in front of the dorm at the heart of the campus, jamming all kinds of music. It was like that night had a soundtrack of its own. 2Pac's album *Me Against the World* had just come out. His song "So Many Tears" had a bass line that was recognizable for miles and is indelibly etched into my brain from that night. Anyone who had any kind of bass in their ride wanted to jam that track to demonstrate their trunk rattle. Pac was so popular back then that his album was played almost in its entirety because virtually every car was jamming one of these tracks. Me against the world would be an appropriate title for what I was to experience at UT and subsequently society as a whole. UT was truly a microcosm of life to come, making it an excellent training ground for a young Black kid who had aspirations of success in a world where not many of the successful look like him. Only fifteen CEOs in the history of Fortune 500 companies have ever been Black. Would I be number sixteen or would I fall short of that aspiration and be relegated to whatever boundaries society proposed that I play within?

I remember the first time I was pulled over by Austin police. I wasn't driving. I was a passenger, one of three passengers. The driver was Mexican, and myself and the two other passengers were Black. The car was an old Malibu Capri. It was somewhere around 1:00 a.m. We were probably coming back from Sixth Street or something. Who knows? College students driving around at that time of night wasn't uncommon. That part of Austin is frequented by students who take a much-needed break from academic pursuits to blow off a little steam. I've always been raised to respect the police and to be extremely cooperative, not out of fear but just pure respect and the idea that they're here to protect us. I didn't feel very protected that night. I felt discriminated. We were pulled over and asked a series of questions that were at best repetitive and clearly incendiary and condescending. When asked where we were going, we responded by saying that we were going to our dorm. "Yeah, right" was his response. He followed by asking what school we attended. I guess to try to catch us in our collective lie. "UT." His response was a chuckle followed by a "wait here." Clearly, a car full of minorities, traveling in a beat-up sedan, couldn't attend one of the top schools in the nation. We were most likely in route to find a place to do drugs or find a car that was appealing enough for us to steal. He came back to the car to return my buddy's license and simply said, "Go home." He walked away and drove off. The four of us sent him off with a one-finger salute as he was driving away of course. Ain't nobody got time to go to jail!

My relationship with APD evolved after that. Those guys I was in the car with dropped out of UT, and I joined a fraternity—Alpha Phi Alpha. I was proud of my frat, proud of its origin, proud of the history, and proud of the guys I was associated with. Let me be clear in saying that Alpha Phi Alpha is a nonhazing fraternity, but since the statute of limitations for me and the distinguished gentlemen involved in the fraternity at that time have expired, I can say that we pledged for exactly four weeks, five days, three hours, forty-two minutes, and twenty-two seconds. The duration is not what matters. Some have pledged much longer, some shorter. What I've found is that the adversity through which you have come has a distinct relationship with the bonds that were formed with the line brothers and your ability to withstand adversity in the future. APD was a frequent visitor at Alpha parties. Sometimes, it was because of noise violations. Sometimes, it was because they were patrolling the area on Sixth Street where we happened to be and they stopped by. Other times, we invited them to our party to proactively address any complaints of disruption. I actually became friendly with them and built relationships with them so that when problems arose, I knew the officers who would respond to the incident. We'd have a cordial conversation, come to an agreement, and then move on about our evenings. It was quite a contrast from the condescending incident in the Malibu Capri.

A proper pledge process is also steeped in history, meaning and depth. It is not a competition to determine one's alcohol tolerance or limitations of being able to be demeaned. It is about replicating life, past, present, and future, in a condensed amount of time to prepare men for what is to come by educating them on what has happened and by equipping them with tools and networks that will be beneficial in the future. I developed an even stronger affinity for learning about the historical context that Black men and women faced in the early 1900s in Ithaca, New York, and elsewhere. There is a reason we lined up from shortest to tallest. It wasn't because it looked cool. It was because my ancestors believed the best way to look out for each other was to be able to see over the person's head in front of you. I won't say that the fraternity was all about high-minded history and prestigious legacy. We partied our asses off. We did some things that we will never publicly admit to. It's interesting though. As my tenure in the frat grew, I began to feel more and more like the Black Greek system was more of an educated system of gangs or a system put in place that evolved into another method to segregate and embattle Black people. An interesting question, however, is, Was it perpetuated by an outside force, or did we do it to ourselves? Did we become so intoxicated by immense and all-consuming pride in our own respective organizations that we somehow forgot that we were all fighting common battles? The struggle was never supposed to be Alphas versus Kappas or Ques or AKAs versus Deltas. The struggle was supposed to be Black men and women versus a society of oppression that raged against us to keep us divided and therefore weakened.

There's a biblical story regarding the Tower of Babel and the diversification of languages. It is said that at one time, the entire world spoke the same language and were able to accomplish many fantastic things because of their ability to unite such a large mass. Most everything was possible because of their homogeneity of language and their diversity of origin. As the story goes, one day, the people decided to build a city and, in that city, a tower that could reach Heaven. God decided to diversify the language, creating an inherent barrier and hardship that limited their ability and created differences that were highlighted and augmented to weaken the group. No longer could they accomplish what they could before. They scattered to multiple areas around the group. Did we create our own Tower of Babel through this system of fraternities and sororities, or was there a system of oppression at play that stoked the fires of divisiveness? I don't regret my decision to join a frat, and I firmly believe that when applied with their original intent, they are an agent for great community service and activities for many causes, not just ones facing the Black community. Historically, Black Greek organizations are now vastly diversified. I personally brought in one of my fraternity brothers of the fairer shade, and I love him to this day. There is room for each fraternity and sorority, but I implore us to reserve space for collective action around issues that plague our entire community so that we can leverage the power of the mass, speaking as one to accomplish fantastic things.

There were many secrets that were shared during my pledge process related to my fraternity, Egyptology, and what seemed to be a bit of mysticism wrapped in rituals. I will not divulge those secrets, in this format or in any other, just as stories were passed through my ancestors who were enslaved years ago. We never wrote anything down but instead provided this secret education through the spoken word only. I'm sure there were multiple reasons for that. One of which is to keep some semblance of privacy and secrets among themselves.

DIAGNOSIS
[dieg-noses]

Definition: The identification of the nature of an illness or other problem by examination of the symptoms

> *Political extremism involves two prime ingredients: an excessively simple diagnosis of the world's ills, and a conviction that there are identifiable villains back of it all.*
> —John W. Gardner

Understanding and analyzing the symptoms of a problem lead to a diagnosis, but it's often met with conflicting emotions. One can no longer claim ignorance but must instead make the conscious decision to either willfully ignore something wrong or commit to solving a problem with an unpredictable solution.

CHAPTER 5

You Got Yours, But the Battle Ain't Over

Systems of Oppression

What Black and Brown people have been experiencing over hundreds of years is systemic. This systemic approach created generations of people who were products of the programming done by people who intended to create a hierarchy of humans or a caste system that would divide the privileged from the impoverished. Having been discouraged to educate ourselves and instead forced to work with our hands produced generations of strong laborers. Our hands, our backs, and our wills are strong. However, we lack the commensurate academic fortitude necessary to advance beyond the field. No, we're not dumb. It is quite the contrary. We rise despite the fact that we have been, and in some ways continue to be, systematically oppressed. My point is that if the majority of the wealth in America is owned by the wealthiest 1 percent, how much of the 1 percent is Black? I'm proud that we've been able to acquire wealth in a number of ways. I'm proud of our advances in athletics, entertainment, entrepreneurship, medicine, law, etc. We are phenomenal, but we're still behind our counterparts from other cultures. Let's dig deeper into the wealth patterns of Black people. How many Black people have acquired wealth from being CEO of a major company? How many Black people have become wealthy from professional sports? How many Black people have become wealthy from medicine or law? Do we leverage our physical abilities and artistic talents to gain wealth more than demonstrating our intellectual prowess? Perhaps. But why?

I remember when it became public knowledge that Lawrence Taylor, hall of fame linebacker for the New York Giants, couldn't read. This guy, a professional football player, one of the best to ever play the game, was passed from grade to grade through the educational system because he possessed the strength and skill to dominate on the field. I don't blame LT for his inability to read. I blame a system of oppression that applauded the athlete and discouraged the academician. On some levels, one could argue that Black people are free to entertain the American people. We can play on the field and on the court, but we're limited in the front office. I live in Houston where our professional football team had a Black GM. I'm proud of that fact and proud of Rick Smith for having achieved that post. I'd love to see more of that. I'd love to see a Black NFL team owner. Perhaps that would have changed the conversation around the Colin Kaepernick kneel. Ultimately, Colin's initiative evolved into teams kneeling during the national anthem, which was manipulated and taken out of context, positioning NFL players who kneeled as being anti-American flag (read anti-American). This issue was never about being anti-anything. Mr. Kaepernick and his fellow NFL players were kneeling to raise awareness to the inequalities that persist when it comes to some police officers around the country and minorities. Without a voice in those NFL owners' meetings, this point of clarity is lost, and the conversation remains due to what could have been called an intentional distraction to the issue.

Again, awareness was raised through a very public stage with no tangible results. There was talk that the NFL would change their policy, forcing players to stand during the national anthem. President Trump's sound bite, when speaking about NFL players who knelt during the national anthem, was close to becoming a reality when he once said, "Wouldn't you love to see one of these NFL owners, when someone disrespect our flag, to say, 'Get that son of a bitch off the field right now. Out! He's fired. He's fired!'" On this day in Alabama, during a rally for a republican senator Luther Strange, President Donald Trump distracted the entire country from the truth of the purpose of "the kneel." Intentional or not, the forty-fifth president of the United States perpetuated a system of oppression by changing the conversation to a sensationalized hot topic instead of giving ear to a segment of the population by addressing long-standing inequalities. The best way to derail a movement in America that lacks popularity with the majority is to label it "anti-American." No one wants to be seen in this light. This reminds me of the time period in America in the late 1940s and early 1950s when McCarthyism ran rampant and President Truman ordered federal service workers to be tested for "loyalty" by executive order. We're not quite to that level of overt oppression, but an administration that threatens first amendment rights through maligning itself with the media and with organizations and movements who have a dissimilar perspective puts our country on a dangerous path.

Imagine the power that is yet to be harnessed when combining a physically strong body, finely tuned artistic talents, and a well-informed mind. Examples of this power have been manifested in people who have moved from the talent performing on stage to being the leader of the record label deciding which talent performs on stage. I applaud both the talent and hustle of the entertainer and the business acumen of the executive that determines the entertainment. I'm happy to see us succeed on any level, but I urge us to keep pressing toward the highest levels of autonomy, authority, and wealth.

The Man Who Came Back

Recently, Jas and I watched a movie that I had the privilege to be a part of in May of 2007. Despite the limited release, and even more limited success, of the film, it was the highlight of my acting career. I worked with people that I'd admired for years like Billy

Zane, George Kennedy, Armand Assante, and Eric Braeden. Yes, my mother made me watch soap operas when I was growing up because we only had one television in the house, so I knew all about *Victor* and *The Young and the Restless*.

The movie was called *The Man Who Came Back* and was based on the Thibodaux Massacre in 1887. Approximately sixty Black people were slaughtered because they refused to work on plantations for practically nothing in a postslavery society. Portrayed from the perspective of the White overseer, Eric's character Reese Paxton, the movie endeavors to highlight the societal injustices surrounding plantation workers in Louisiana. It depicted a lack of basic human rights for Black people and disgust for Black sympathizers. My character, Richmond, was the servant of the crooked Judge Duke, played by the late Academy Award winner George Kennedy. Mr. Kennedy was a great guy to work with. I appreciate the few conversations that we had and found him to be a consummate professional. Armand Assante and Eric Braeden were both intense actors on the set. I enjoyed watching them prepare for scenes and release their creativity and intensity once the director called for action. I learned so much just by watching the way they navigated scenes and played off the energy of the other actors. Billy Zane was one of the most down-to-earth guys I'd ever met. He's the kind of guy you'd love to have a beer with and just listen to stories of experiences that he's had throughout his career. They were all decent guys once the day wrapped, but while we were working, we all stepped back in time to a period of great violence and evil.

The movie is difficult to watch. It brings audiences into the vile world of White dominance and human injustice. Opposers to the White majority, Black or White, were regarded as less than human and treated accordingly. Rape, murder, and gross inequities were common and widely accepted. While Black people struggled to survive in a post-Civil War, postslavery America, they were constantly faced with atrocities that prohibited any semblance of progression. The plantation workers in the movie were depicted as hardworking, yet they were paid in "script" or fake money that was only valid at the store on the plantation where prices were extremely inflated. They had no opportunity to advance and no opportunity to save money to perhaps start their own business or buy land or build any kind of future for their families. Their past, present, and future were dictated by White men who were only interested in self-advancement.

Despite investing sweat equity and blood into building the foundations of this country, Black people have yet to yield a commensurate return. No, I'm not suggesting that we receive reparations. I'm suggesting that we have appropriate representation in politics to impact federal and local legislation that impacts minority communities. I'm suggesting that those of us who have influence or authority in various industries create opportunities for minorities, of all kinds, and do so with the mindset of investing in our own communities. I'm suggesting that we teach our children to not only study to get an education that affords them the opportunity to be productive and successful citizens but that we teach them to strive for independence and empowerment to better serve those that are less fortunate. We can no longer settle for the crab in the bucket mentality that encourages people to advance on the backs of others and to pull down those that may advance before us. We must elevate ourselves while pulling up others behind us and pushing up those ahead of us. We must leverage our individual advancements to create momentum and opportunities for our collective progression.

Jas asked me if it was difficult to do the movie. Honestly, most days, it wasn't. I was infatuated by the lights and the set design. It was truly a great experience for me as an actor. Before that, my acting career consisted of commercials, short films, and corporate training videos. I was tired of being the guy in the Popeyes chicken commercial enjoying a spicy drumstick and the creepy guy on training videos that learned a lesson about sexual harassment after making lewd jokes about Becky from accounting. I was a little starstruck as well. I felt like I was among a community of artists that strove to create moving motion pictures to tell stories of great relevance. I had my own trailer, with snacks! What? Craft services was on point! My speaking parts were cut from the movie, but I took advantage of the Perrier and mixed Planters nuts.

Then there were other days where I was reminded that I was Black and that my history and the history of my ancestors in this country are nowhere near glamorous. The stark realization of my pedigree was made clear when Reese Paxton brings the body of one of the plantation workers into the local saloon. I was there as the dutiful servant of Judge Duke, standing behind attending to his beck and call. Reese found the body hanging in the woods following the departure of the group after declaring a strike. The body was that of the leader of the strike, Winton, played by J. D. Hawkins. Reese sought justice for the man but only found himself framed for his murder. He was operating under the fallacy that America provides liberty and justice for all. That's not so much the case. It never has been. Liberty and justice have been reserved for those who have power, influence, money, or all of the above. Some might say that's a cynical perspective, but there is an abundance of evidence in court cases where the lack of privilege and power has made lady liberty blind in instances where she should have had her eyes wide open to false accusations and tampered evidence. Let's face it. Power and privilege have been historically bestowed to White people. I am not saying that every White person has a safe full of gold bars in their personal treasury at home, but statistically speaking, minorities tend to disproportionately make up the prison population. Even though Black people represent only 13 percent of the total US population, almost 50 percent of the people exonerated are Black. Why is that? Perhaps it has something to do with the fact that almost 40 percent of the prison population is Black. Perhaps it has something to do with under- or inadequate representation of Black people in the criminal justice system. Perhaps it has something to do with a phenomenon called "own-race bias" that has shown to incorrectly accuse innocent Black men of crimes they didn't commit because the accuser couldn't distinguish racially distinct features separate from the attacker. Reese Paxton shows us that liberty and justice have never been for all, and I'd argue that we continue to struggle for equality.

As I look back at my character now, I realize that I personify the lackadaisical attitudes of many in the minority community. Richmond had a decent existence, was well dressed, and was "comfortable" inside the quarters of the judge. His people were relegated to fieldwork in the blistering sun, toiling for hours on end with little respite. They wore tattered clothes and scraped together an existence. Even after seeing Winton's body in the saloon, Richmond remained silent. It wasn't until the end of the movie (spoiler alert) that Richmond abandons the judge, left to deal with the vengeance-filled Reese Paxton. My character wore nice clothes and was able to shave, and even though he was belittled, he didn't have to work in the elements. He was of a slightly higher status, and because of that, he stayed silent. Richmond didn't wield the whip that cracked the backs of his brothers and sisters, but he did nothing to prevent it. I'm sure it was out of fear for his life, fear for his family, and fear for his station in life. Richmond didn't want to mess a good thing up. Sound familiar? When we find our place of success in life, decide to stay silent, and sit idle as others who look like us are being unfairly and unjustly treated, we share the guilt of the persecutors. Enough is enough. There is no great White hope coming for us to save our people and to hand out forty acres and a mule. We are no longer beholden to oblige slave owners, and we have the capability to mobilize our communities to influence the nation and impact change. Our voice lies not in the perpetuation of stereotypes, or in the pursuit of individual accolades, but in our ability to stand united with each other to advocate for programs and resources that matter to us.

CHAPTER 6

Love Unexpected, Love Forbidden, and Love Unending

I Didn't Know I Was Thirsty

She was like no other woman that I had ever met. Her style and sophistication were in a class of their own. The first time I saw her, she stole my breath and captivated my attention. It was like walking into a museum to see the Hope Diamond. I know the diamond exists, but I have never laid eyes on it, and I wouldn't dare get close enough to touch it, much less possess it. I kept my distance but secretly was in awe by this woman. I found her to be charming, intelligent, ambitious, and exotically beautiful.

"Hi, I'm Jasmine. It's nice to meet you."

"Nice to meet you too."

I tried to play it cool.

Growing up as a kid who attended mostly Black schools, I didn't have much exposure to a diverse range of women. It wasn't until my time in Austin at the University of Texas in the mid to late nineties that I gained an appreciation for women of different cultures. I still loved Black women, but I found myself intrigued by women from around the globe. It was like the UN was on my college campus, and I had the opportunity to meet and interact with women from various countries in the world, like Eritrea, Egypt, Saudi Arabia, etc. One of my best friends was from Persia or Iran as it's now called. I had never seen women who looked like this. For some reason, foreign cultures have always been appealing to me. I started taking French lessons when I was in the sixth grade. I loved it. I loved the language, I loved the culture, and I fell in love with the idea of appreciating that which is different and beautiful in its own way. It's a wonder I fell in love with the language because my teacher was "Le Hot Mess." She opted to forego a bra and instead wear her skirts really high on her stomach and use a really wide belt to provide some measure of bolstering to her supersized boobs. It looked like she was smuggling a large loaf of French bread in her shirt every day. It was not cute. Nevertheless, I stayed the course and took French throughout high school and college. I competed in French-speaking competitions when I was in high school. I couldn't get enough of this foreign culture. For some reason, I've always been drawn to the exotic.

Even though I had this newfound exposure, I didn't take a deep dive into dating someone who was non-Black. Honestly, I was scared. I had never done that before. I may have wanted to, but anticipation of stares and whispers of "sellout" ran through my mind. I remember hearing people say, "Oh, he gotta get a White woman now that he's making money." It was like, at once, a symbol of success and a crimson mark of shame for selecting someone of a different racial background to love. I wasn't quite ready for that. I also didn't know if I was "White girl attractive" or if I was (insert another culture) girl attractive. I was so insecure back in the day that some days, I didn't even feel like I was Black girl attractive, but I thought I had a shot with them since they were "supposed" to hook up with Black guys. They had some level of perceived obligation to date Black guys. I quickly found that to be a fallacy as well. No one is obligated to love anyone, and people should be free to follow their souls not the box they check on applications for ethnicity. But still, though it was many years ago, stories like that of Emmett Till still rung loudly in the minds of Black men at that time.

In 1955, a fourteen-year-old Emmett decided to whistle at an attractive White lady. He was brutally murdered and tossed in the

Tallahatchie River with a cotton gin fan tied to his neck with barbed wire for that expression of admiration. while lynchings weren't commonplace in the nineties, remnants of racism still littered our collective psyche. I dated a young lady of the Caucasian persuasion for a brief period of time. She was cool to hang out with and a supersweet person. Her mom really liked me. Unfortunately, her grandfather was still a practicing member of a Ku Klux Klan chapter in a small town in Texas. Uh, bye Felecia. That romance quickly faded for a number of reasons, one of which being that I didn't want the Klan's robes to clash with her wedding dress, and I didn't need a burning cross at the church to let the guests know where to park. I'm good.

Jasmine and I lost contact for a few years, but then life brought us crashing back together. We began to work together, so we spent more and more time in each other's space. We didn't plan on it, but we learned a lot about each other. She gained a greater appreciation for me and I for her. That appreciation evolved into admiration over time. Our hearts were pulling toward each other. It was like my soul remembered her from a different lifetime and was struggling to reconnect. We share so many interests, aspirations, and philosophies. We have a similar worldview, even a similar style. The only problem was that I was married at the time. I try to think back to myself to remember if there was a point where I could have stopped my feelings from progressing, and it all seems like a blur. My soul clung to a beautiful Indian woman who had a very traditional family. I certainly didn't fit their prototype for her husband. The stereotype demands that I be an Indian doctor who comes from a long line of scholars, preferably a Jatt Sikh. I'm a Black guy from the south side of Houston, who earned every accolade and pulled himself up from living three houses down from a crack house. I'm nowhere near their preferred pedigree. I can't imagine the struggle that Kamala Harris's parents went through. Consider the adversity that an Indian mom and a Jamaican father experienced when they fell in love during the height of the civil rights movement. Kamala was the product of a taboo relationship, and she turned out to be pretty successful. Maybe one of our kids will go on to be a rock star prosecutor and politician.

My previous marriage wasn't taboo at all, but it was emotionally over. We were trudging through the doldrums of life, looking for the next day to be better than the last. We left each other wanting and didn't know how to effectively articulate our needs despite counseling, prayer, and unwanted interventions from friends. We became roommates, who shared the responsibilities of managing a household. I can't tell you the exact day we transitioned to that status. It was a gradual evolution like a single stream of water persistently flowing through the same spot over time to create a chasm between two bodies of land. Even though we lived in the same space, I couldn't have felt farther away. I was broken and empty, and I didn't know how to bridge the gap to allow her back into my life. Our love languages weren't compatible, which created constant emotional miscommunication. We just left our respective vessels, wanting more. The reality is I didn't know how dead I was inside until I saw life in Jasmine when I first met her.

I never meant to cause anyone pain, but I did. I listened to my soul. Honestly, I tried to stop, but life wouldn't let me. There was such a struggle within me to leave her alone and to remain just coworkers. There were so many nights that I'd be racked with guilt for even thinking about her. I've not had the greatest track record with relationships. I'll admit that. I didn't want to be another divorce statistic, and I didn't want to abandon my morality. I was raised in the church and not just in a "I got dragged to church every Sunday by my mama" kind of way. I mean I really enjoyed it! I would have mini sermons in my apartment in college because I was so engulfed in the church culture and desired the closest relationship possible with God. I taught Sunday school in one of the most prominent churches in Houston for God's sake! There was no pun intended. I had a reputation for being an advocate for strong marriages and stable families! I wasn't looking for an opportunity to totally wreak havoc on my world.

To try to avoid the impending hell, I divulged the details of my struggle to other men and women in an attempt to have support to "get back on track" despite being a fiercely private person. In my desperation, I exposed my weaknesses and deepest secrets to friends, parishioners, professional counselors, and family members. I remember taking a walk with someone whom I called a friend, who said everything we discussed was confidential, "just between us." I learned that confidentiality clause didn't include his wife, who took the liberty to divulge my shared vulnerabilities with my ex. My "support system" was woefully flawed. Every morning, I'd awake with such extreme angst and stress that I'd go about my day with the weight of two worlds on my shoulders. Sleep would never come quickly enough. It was the only escape from my anguish, and it was at best ephemeral. The next morning, I'd awake to the same nightmare. I hated my life, I hated myself, and I hated God for allowing me to get in this situation.

Thoughts of my ex, my son, my ex's family, and my family would race through my head. How would my actions impact these other people? I had no desire to create emotional or financial instability for my ex, nor did I want to give my son any additional reasons to have feelings of rejection or inadequacy. The thought of spending a minute, much less full-time custody, without my son made me physically ill. Since his birth, he has been a huge part of my life, and I knew I'd miss our one-on-one times together. He and I had a nightly ritual. We'd start with bath time that was composed of wrestling while the tub filled with water, playtime and a quick wash in the tub, and drying him off as quickly as possible so I could get clothes on his shivering little body because he's so temperature sensitive. I knew I'd miss our nighttime reading and "superhero prayers." This was our thing, just him and me.

I had no desire to turn the world as I knew it upside down, but circumstances kept pushing Jasmine and me closer together. Eventually, I fell in love with her. I didn't want to lose my son, my church, my friends, my home, and my financial stability. I even dreaded losing some of my ex's family members, but I knew that if we divorced, I'd be marginalized and vilified. I was right. There was only one guy from her family that ever reached out to me to say, "Hey, shit happens. We still cool." To a guy that was so depressed and disappointed in himself to the point of borderline suicide, this person's words were worth more than every dollar I paid to counselors and every minute I spent listening to churchgoers, who advised me to "just keep praying and trust God."

This has not been an easy road to travel. This has been nothing short of driving head first into a kerosene-soaked road, set ablaze for an undetermined distance, with the expectation that I'll not perish in the fire but will instead be purified and refined.

I have apologized for the pain I caused and accepted account-ability for my contribution to the demise of that relationship. My sincere wish is that we dust off the ashes from the past and move toward a future with resurrected life and love. Inshallah.

Needless to say, I went through six layers of hell as I went through my divorce. When I would swap stories with my boys about our ex's and I would share the crazy stuff I was going through, they would always say, "Dude, your ex has mine beat! I gotta make sure she doesn't give my ex any ideas." That wasn't a contest I wished to win. A Black woman will enlist the help from every other bitter Black woman in the beauty shop to figure out ways to live vicariously through her, envisioning every guy that ever did them wrong, to roy-ally screw you over. I can't even tell you the crazy stuff that happened to me. Well, I can, but there's no need to bring up the past in a negative light. Let's just say that my life became a Lifetime Channel miniseries, complete with alter egos, espionage, and legal drama. I guess any woman would behave similarly, regardless of cultural back-ground. Every scorned woman has at least two crazy women in their corner, who gives them great ideas about "what they would do if it were them."

As a man would travel across a dessert to reach the spring for which he has been searching, so will that same man endure the onslaught of malice and defamation that's levied by the scorned woman. I didn't know that I was thirsty until I found Jasmine.

Sometime after my divorce, Jas and I, we were hanging out in Austin for a random weekend. We did it on a whim. The week was hectic for us, and we just needed relief from the drama that was constantly unfolding and persistently escalating in our lives. Austin is one of my favorite places in Texas because the atmosphere is eclec-tic and accepting. We wouldn't stick out like a sore thumb to be stared at like a three-eyed circus freak. Either we would blend into the landscape without a second look or we'd be applauded for our courage to love each other in the face of racism. My most fond memory from that weekend was when we were hanging out at a restaurant on Rainey Street, enjoying a few drinks on the patio, and a random woman stopped by our table as a sea of people paraded past the restaurant. She was young, probably in her mid- to late twenties with blond hair, cutoff jean shorts, and the obligatory Birkenstocks. She was walking with a few other people, but she very briefly stopped by to say, "You two look beautiful together." That wasn't the first time that we'd heard that sentiment, but on that particular weekend, it was like a splash of fresh water to both of our faces. We needed that. We needed to hear that someone found us beautiful despite our feelings of self-loathing and uncertainty. We needed to feel like we had a place somewhere in society that would see past our pain to embrace our value. Graciously, we thanked the woman as she offered a kind smile and continued on.

Another highlight of that weekend was sitting down at Pelon's Tex Mex on Red River Street, waiting for a concert to start at Stubb's. It was the first time that we had an opportunity to just exist. We stayed at a nearby hotel, so we took advantage of our location and walked around downtown Austin. There's a certain charm to downtown despite the abundance of homeless people who frequent a shelter in the area. Pelon's has fantastic margaritas and offers outdoor seating on a slightly elevated patio. One of the most noticeable landmarks at the restaurant is an oak tree that is so organically beautiful that it looks like it could have been sculpted. Its branches extend toward the sky and over the rooftop as if to frame Pelon's, presenting a work of art to God. It's pretty cool. We were enjoying the occasional breeze and Tex Mex as we sat on the patio. I look over at Jas as she takes a sip of her margarita and notice her eyes looking at me over the top of her glass. She had been observing me for a while. She was so accustomed to seeing angst on my face that it was nice for her to get a glimpse of peace and contentment. More than drinking her margarita, she drank from hope's spring as she was able to recognize peace within herself as well. For a brief moment, we were behind the rushing waters of an imaginary waterfall in that secluded cave just beyond the world outside. It was our intimate moment where we were able to drown out all judgments about our relationship from society, all cultural expectations, and all religious pretexts that typically pervaded our thoughts.

Relationships are difficult for a variety of reasons, most of which have nothing to do with the two people involved in the relationship. Each person has an exponential number of relationships and past experiences that often make an appearance, sometimes for an extended stay, in the course of a relationship. Probably chief of those relationships are those that we share with our parents. Whether we like it or not, we often expect the woman of our dreams to be like the best parts of our mother. She should be loving despite our numerous faults, and she should be nurturing, taking care of our every anticipated need. She should be beautiful from the time she wakes up in the morning until the time she goes to sleep. And above all, she should never be moody. Women expect their guy to the best parts of their father. The guy must be strong; protective; loving; financially stable; attractive; able to notice changes in hairstyle, clothing, nail polish, and jewelry; able to remember the details of every encounter throughout the course of your relationship; and at all times on their side. These are just the prerequisites. There are many more attributes that we desire in the perfect mate, but these provide us with a decent baseline. Now, let's imagine that we find these mythical unicorns and decide to integrate them into our lives. The first question that often enters our minds is, What will my family think? How will Mom or Dad react? How will my brother, sister, favorite uncle, or play cousin react? We tend to include, and often worry about, the opinions of others and for good reason. They can help us see beyond our rose-colored glasses to identify potential red flags. Sometimes, the issues are so glaring that they've gone beyond red flags and are neon signs that say, "Stay away from her crazy ass. She's a stalker," or "Girl, you know he's broke. That's his mama's car!" Sometimes, we're so infatuated with a person that it's hard to see things that are obvious to others. But what if there are no red flags and our loved ones' criticism is based in fear. They're afraid that our life choices are too contradictory to Sam's paradigm or too contradictory to man's interpretation of God's Words. Man tends to weaponize and politicize God's intentions for man's own gain. Religious leaders have used God to control and manipulate people since there was an acknowledgment of the Almighty. While God extends infinite love and abounding grace, man sits in judgment, awaiting the opportunity to highlight his own piety at the expense of another. I really think there should be a commandment that says, "Thou shalt not be a jerk in the name of the church." Fear and judgment often prevent us from seeing beauty in the misunderstood.

"You're gonna lose him."

The role that my oldest brother Bob played in integrating Jas cannot be overstated. He helped other members of my family see that my relationship with Jas was an awakening of my independence from other peoples' expectations of me and not fleeting relationship. At some point in a person's life, he or she has to decide if they will continue to live for the approval of others or if they will live a life that invigorates themselves every morning they are blessed to see the sun rise on God's green earth. One must decide if they will let their contributions to society, and those less fortunate, stand for their merit instead of perpetually remembering pains of the past that prohibit forward momentum. Marc Antony has a song called "Vivir Mi Vida." Live my life. Listening to that song, even today, gives me goose bumps and almost brings me to tears. What resonates with me is that fact that for so long, I haven't lived my life. I've lived the life that others have wanted me to live. Even when I tried to break free from the norm, I was dragged back by the foundations of culture and religion that at one time provided stability but now serve to enslave and restrict me from embracing the man that God created me to be.

"You're gonna lose him if you keep acting like this. If you love him, just be there for him. Accept him for who he is and for who he loves. Period. He's a grown man. Let him live his own life." This was part of the conversation that Bob had with several members of my family in preparation for a get-together at his house. He knew that some of them had a problem with my relationship and that I rejected their disapproval. I understood their concerns, but I wasn't about to change my convictions. Through his orchestration, Jas was introduced to the family, and now, my mom very conscientiously approaches Jasmine at every family gathering to say how much she appreciates her influence in my life.

Jasmine has been water to parched lips. She loves me in a way that no other woman has. She expands my mind and fills my heart with an abundance of love. Most of the time, her words are tender even though she sometimes pulls out the Punjabi auntie, who threatens to "beat me with a shoe" in a manufactured thick Indian accent. Most of the time, I deserve it. Her consideration of me, to ensure that my needs are met, is refreshing, from the simplistic expression of making me a sandwich before going to the airport for a business trip to coordinating an elaborate surprise for my birthday to include college friends, burlesque dancers, and high-end Italian shoes. She awakens my soul in a way that feels familiar, in a very déjà vu kind of way. Her elegance is enchanting, and her benevolence is inspiring. This woman is my partner. This woman represents my freedom. This woman checks every box for me, including those that I didn't know that I had. May our relationship inspire conversations about cultural integration and diversity that create a global impact. Inshallah.

CHAPTER 7

Love Ain't Easy, But It's Worth the Effort

Accepting Jas's Love

I'm not accustomed to being taken care of. Normally, I'm the rock of the relationship. I cook, I clean, I work, and I have historically made the higher salary. I've taken care of domestic duties inside and outside of the house. I remember when Bryce was born I made sure that I took more than my share of feeding times throughout the night despite being in graduate school when he was a newborn. I remember many nights when I held him in my left arm like a running back heading toward the end zone with a bottle strategically placed in his mouth with my left hand while simultaneously typing with my right hand as I worked on a paper for my MBA. I did what I had to do in previous relationships to keep the logistics going. I'm good at that. I'm actually too good at that because I have difficulty accepting help. I sacrifice my time so that others may rest as a demonstration of my love. It's just what I do. I serve others.

Jas is the first woman, besides my mom, who has ever served me. She willfully assumes the responsibility of caring for me in many different ways. One evening after taking a shower, she offered to put lotion on my back. Unfortunately, I was bestowed with the skin of a south Texas alligator. When we first started dating, my back was literally scaly. It was dry and flaky and at times painful. She prioritized applying lotion to my back almost every night we were together. One night, after putting lotion on my back, she asked me to sit down on the bed. You know what my mind was thinking? *All right now, don't start nothing you can't finish!* Okay, I'm a guy. Of course, I think that all roads lead to sex. She swung my legs on the bed and placed my feet on her lap as she sat down as well. She began to massage my bare feet with lotion, caressing them and kneading them with her fingers. Every neuron in my body was firing. I, at once, had feelings of discomfort and euphoria. No one had ever massaged my feet before. No one had ever touched my feet before. My feet will never grace any fashion magazines to model flip-flops. They are definitely working feet. They are feet that reflect years of yard work, walking, running, weight lifting, and general neglect. My feet aren't quite at the stage where little children scream in horror when I take my socks off, but I guarantee the ladies in the nail shop would have a field day talking about me if I tried to get a pedicure. "Oh, we're gonna need the industrial tools for these!"

I didn't know how to respond to this. I felt like I needed to massage her feet. Reciprocity was the first thing I thought of. I've always been the giver, not the receiver. This was weird. Not only was it weird, it was a small sample of the overall theme of our relationship. She takes care of me in many ways beyond a simple foot rub or preparation of my dinner. She proactively thinks of ways to make me comfortable, to make me feel special, and to provide a welcoming environment to me. She thinks about the little things that make a big impact. She knows I love the smell of eucalyptus, so she buys me eucalyptus hand lotion to keep in my car to use when I need it, which is frequent. Remember, my alligator DNA doesn't stop at my back. Those things probably appear minuscule, but the thoughts behind her actions are massive. I'm still learning to just be loved without feeling an obligation of reciprocity. My demonstrations of love are not compulsory. They are 100 percent voluntary as I thank my lucky stars that she chose to share a life with me.

Interracial Love and Challenges

"You couldn't find a Black woman you like." "Oh, you think you're too good for a Black woman now that you have a little money?" "You know all Black people are lazy, don't you? He's not good enough for you. Why don't you find a good Indian doctor or engineer?" People don't typically say this to our faces, but you can believe that their stares speak volumes. We walk into the most benign places like a restaurant, a gym, or some random department store and for the most part, people are cool. We live in the fourth largest city in the country, so we're somewhat progressive in our area. But every now and then, we get the stare of shame as if to say, "How dare we decide to fall in love with someone outside our race?"

These stares of judgment often occur in the most unexpected places. The parents of children who are athletes typically have a special bond because you spend so much time together at practice or the actual sporting event itself. Clearly, you have something in common because you're both there supporting your kids, you're both there spending a ton of money on whatever sport they've selected, and you both have pancake butt from sitting on the bleachers made from lumber procured from hell's darkest forest. You obviously have things to talk about even if you fall back on your safety net of talking about the kids.

The moms typically form a network to keep each other abreast of changes in schedules, practice times, competition times, uniforms to wear for the meet, etc. Ava, Jas's daughter and my bonus daughter, competes in gymnastics. She's incredibly talented and probably one of the most naturally gifted kids on the team. Yes, I know I'm biased, but I'm also incredibly tough when it comes to setting kids' expectations. I don't believe that everyone should get a trophy and everyone is not a winner. I believe that it's okay if my kid sucks at something. I'll be the first to make that known. Why waste time, and why set your kid up for crushing disappointment in the future because you've been drowning them in butterfly kisses and false hope? If they suck, they suck. That frees them to find their true gift, or it presses them to fight harder to be better. But I digress.

Jas noticed Ava talking to another little girl on the team. She was an adorable little Black girl with the cutest smile. Her mother, a Black woman with natural braids cascading from the crown of her head, waited in the common area of the gym a bit to herself. Jas decided to initiate a conversation that was unfortunately painstaking. There's no clearer indication of someone who doesn't want to talk to you than someone who is responding with one-word answers. It was like she was answering a mandatory questionnaire for compliance training at work on the last day of the deadline.

By the end of the conversation, the girls had been dismissed from practice. Jas ended the conversation, and we all retreated to the car. After we got in the car, Ava asked, "Why was that lady so rude?" Bella, Jas's other daughter and my other bonus daughter, chimed in, "Yeah, she acted like she had an attitude." At the time, Jas and I just thought she had a dry personality. We know other people who had a perpetually flat affect and just thought that was the case for her. No, it wasn't. We saw her chatting it up, laughing, and talking loudly to some other Black lady in the gym. Later, we noticed she was very cordial and conversant to a group of White ladies waiting in the gym. The common theme here is homogeneity. She had a problem with this Indian woman being with this Black man. Perhaps she knows my ex. Or perhaps she has an ex who left her for an Indian woman. Who knows? Either way, she clearly had a problem with us.

Most of the time, it's not that overt. We were in DC once, and I got the nastiest stare from this Indian man who was a street vendor. It was like I was Harvey Weinstein walking this guy's daughter to the casting couch. Whatever. I'm not a stranger to stares for various reasons. I'm not a stranger to random people being uncomfortable around me. As nice of a guy as I try to be, people have clutched their purses a little more closely around me. They have locked their car doors as I walked by. I've known for years that I live with the burden of being guilty until proven innocent as my brown skin often renders an indictment to many people before I even say a word.

On the other hand, there are occasions where people see Jas and me, and they feel enchanted and drawn to us. There was an occasion in an airport where a random airline employee complimented our energy and proceeded to have a relatively long conversation with us. There's not much time for chitchat when you're checking in busy travelers, but he felt compelled to engage in brief discourse and to recognize the uniqueness of our relationship. There are countless other examples as well, but none more prevalent than the Austin example referenced earlier. Visiting Austin almost twenty years after graduating from the University of Texas was an interesting experience for me. I felt like a mildly conservative paternal figure instead of a sexually frustrated, sexually focused, coed. We watched a parade of people on a normal Saturday afternoon who appeared to be athletes, frat boys, sorority girls, tree huggers, hipsters, weed heads, and hoochies. Apparently, there is a trend in fashion among college girls to wear shorts that are short enough to show "underbun." It's like they help each other get dressed, and one girl asks the other, "Hey, can you see the bottom of my butt cheeks in the shorts? No? Ugh! These are way too long." I felt like every girls' father wanting to tell them to go back home and put some clothes on!

I recognize that Austin is a city that tends to be more progressive, in certain areas, and touts its propensity to be "weird," but I wasn't expecting the admiration that we seemed to receive. The stares during our trip there weren't laced in disdain. They were grounded in kindness and respect. It was as if we were continually being approved, stare after stare. We held hands as we walked around the arboretum area, and we were greeted with smiles and nods. Earlier, I mentioned the young women we encountered on Rainey Street as an example of the reception that we received. I really wasn't expecting that, but I was exceedingly grateful. She had no idea how appreciated her words were at that time. At that time, I wondered, Were we beautiful because we're two relatively attractive people sitting together? Were we beautiful because we were bold enough to love each other in a world that has only recently started to embrace interracial couples in the mainstream media? I remember seeing a Cheerios commercial with an interracial family. It was one of the most powerful commercials I had seen, not because of the product it was selling but because of the unsaid messages by showcasing the many shades of family and love.

I pray that our relationship is a beacon of change and global acceptance. I pray that it facilitates intelligent conversations that lead to greater understanding of cultures that belong to not just us but to other cultures that bear their own set of stigmas and stereotypes.

Couples Therapy

Needless to say, when two divorced people get together, there is a pretty large amount of baggage. In the journey of your life together, you're packing around no less than two jumbo suitcases, two carry-ons, and two personal bags that you've stuffed with years' worth of life experiences and drama that have shaped your perspectives and quite possibly left you a very jaded person. You gotta deal with that if you want a healthy relationship. You can't sweep it under the rug or hide it in the closet. Let's face it. There's no more room in your bulging luggage. It's like being emotionally constipated. Walking around full of feces is never fun, and there's no room to enjoy new experiences.

Jas and I would face many challenges at the beginning of our relationship. The biggest of those challenges would be our own self-perceptions. It's difficult to love someone else when we don't have sufficient love for ourselves. We can have the best of intentions, but until we forgive ourselves for whatever malady, sin, or misunderstanding of the past, we can't fall in love with ourselves. We love out of abundance. We give, anything, out of abundance. Therefore, if we possess nothing, we can give nothing. If we possess a little, we can give a little. If we possess much, we can give much. We must possess the greatest love in the world for ourselves in order to love someone else the way they deserve to be loved. Every person should be so fortunate as to have someone in his or her life whose chief concern is making your every day your best day.

Jas loves me like no other woman has ever loved me. There's a competitive reciprocity that fuels our relationship. She anticipates my needs. She serves me. She supports me professionally and bolsters me emotionally. She pours into me with the right contents to fill, and overflow, my cup. This all caught me by surprise. I wasn't used to this kind of treatment. I was the one who always took care of others. I was the servant, the one who anticipated the needs of others. I didn't know how to accept her love. I honestly felt guilty for just receiving. I'd longed for this kind of relationship but had no idea what to do with it when I got it. I remember her telling me stories of when her mom would make sure her dad was taken care of that when he got home from work, she'd give him a drink and a moment to just relax by himself. She would cook food to his preference and cater to his needs. This may sound old-fashioned to some. It may be a no-brainer to others, but to me, it was a novelty that I was unsure about and clearly uncomfortable with.

We decided to proactively go to couples therapy. We both accepted the fact that we need to tackle some of our issues head on before they become major problems in our relationship. At this phase, we can have productive conversations without years of pain and anger to interfere with communication. We can bring up sensitive issues, gently unpack some of our baggage in front of each, and reveal some of our embarrassing contents. Some of it may have stains, some of it may have holes, some of the contents may be unexpected by the other partner, but it's necessary to be able to share even the darkest parts of yourself to the person you've chosen to share your life. Not only is it imperative to be able to share our past, we need to deal with our past. That's the hard part. It's not enough just to say, "This is who I am. Take it or leave it." The goal is to say, "This is who I am and why I am. Now, let's figure out how to reconcile our pasts so that we can have a good future."

There's a scripture in the Bible that says, "Faith without works is dead." I understand now that love by itself is not enough. It's not enough to be in love with someone. So what? I believe that love without works is dead. Clearly, I'm not the foremost authority at relationships given my track record, but I have to believe that a successful relationship goes beyond love and dives head first into work. Love is the prerequisite. I imagine that in a guy's mind, there should be a checklist that goes something like as follows: Is she fine? Check. Does she look good even when she's not wearing makeup? Check. Is her mama crazy? No. Check. Am I in love? Check. Am I willing to work hard for her, sacrifice for her, have incredibly uncomfortable conversations with her, be vulnerable in front of her, and say I'm sorry even when I don't think I'm wrong? Check.

CHAPTER 8

Blending Families, Mending Hearts

Welcome to Our Home

Integrating families postdivorce is incredibly difficult. My therapist (yes, I have a therapist. Don't judge me. You should probably have one too) said that it takes about five years to become a fully integrated blended family. There are many challenges that arise when blending a family. There are emotions to contend with, there are ex-spouses that may complicate the integration by providing inaccurate (i.e., lying) or inappropriate (i.e., gossip and TMI) information, and let's not forget the good old standard possession order (SPO), which, in the case of parents who are unable to successfully negotiate a possession and access schedule on their own, governs the amount of time the noncustodial parent gets to see his or her children. So it's kind of hard to establish a relationship with a child when the cadence of exposure dictates an alternating weekend schedule and a midweek visit for a few hours, not to mention the fact that you often need to deprogram the kid from the toxic rhetoric they've been infused with for the first twenty-four hours on the weekend. The second twenty-four hours is spent enjoying each other, and the remaining time is spent battling anxiety because the drop-off back to the custodial parent is never a picnic. At best, the exchange between exes, depending on the age of the children, is civil. At worst, it is a trip down memory lane back to the pain of the past in form of passive-aggressive behavior or just down right shitty treatment. Integrating is hard work, and it sucks, but I've seen glimpses of goodness, innocence, and purity in my own situation, and I've seen even better in the lives of those around me in similar scenarios. Ask me in about four years.

The first day I met the girls, Bella and Ava, is a day that I will never forget. I remember walking to the door and being greeted by a handmade card that said, "Welcome to our home." There were pictures inside with smiling faces and rainbows. I kept that card.

When Jas answered the door, I was excited to see her but nervous to meet the girls. I wanted them to like me so badly. They were very pleasant and cordial, but liking me took quite a bit of time and effort on me and Jas's part. Jas would frequently ask them how they were, if they felt comfortable or not, what do you think about this guy, do you think he's nice, etc. She would also say nice things about me to them. She'd brag on my intellect or on the way that I treat her and the way that I make her feel. She helped them to see what she sees in me.

Bella

I've always been very respectful of the girls and their space and would never invade that. So my strategy for gaining their trust was to just be present and to take whatever opportunities arose for bonding. With Bella, it was through schoolwork. She is an excellent student with an amazing work ethic. Getting a ninety-nine or a ninety-eight on a test is like giving her a plate of doughnuts and then knocking them in the floor in front her. Depending on how long they've been down there and if she's at home, she'll still eat them (she really loves doughnuts), but it was almost perfect. I'd be over some evenings after school and would be available to help with homework or projects if she needed. I never took over her work. I guided and challenged her along the way. I wanted to make her stronger. I wanted her to know that she can accomplish anything that she wanted badly enough.

She and I have a cerebral relationship. Over time, we've found our love language with each other, and it has nothing to do with hugging or being all touchy-feely. To anyone except Bella and me, it may even appear that we don't like each other, but that couldn't be farther from the truth. Bella and I play verbal and mental chess every day, all day long. We challenge each other's wisdom about certain things. She tries to be annoying to see what kind of reaction she can get or how long she can get away with something, and I'll do something annoying right back, or I'll completely ignore her, taking away her much-anticipated joy.

Bella loves Taylor Swift. I don't mean that in the "Oh, I get all of Taylor's albums" kind of way. I mean she loves Taylor in the "no one better say anything bad about Taylor or any of Taylor's music because she's a musical genius and deserves to win every award every year for the rest of her life, and anyone who thinks otherwise should crawl back under the rock they came from" kind of way. One time, Jas and I did a parody of Taylor's "Look What You Made Me Do." We changed it to "Look What You Made Me Poo" complete with freestyle lyrics outlining bathroom frequency and duration, farts, bloating, and exploding diarrhea. We thought it was hilarious. Bella got so mad. She was almost in tears. I think she was so mad that she wanted to yell, "I'm gonna kick your ass!" But she's too innocent to say anything like that, but I'm pretty sure she thought it. Nobody messes with Tay-Tay.

I'm thankful for my relationship with Bella-Boo. I know she resisted accepting me for a while because she didn't want to feel like she was betraying her dad. I think she would intentionally bring him up in conversation around me to see my reaction. I never wanted to make it an either/or proposition for the girls. I've always respected their father in their presence and never tried to take his place. I needed the girls to know that, but I couldn't just come out and tell them because that would be too scary for them. So instead, I started bringing him up in conversation. I'd speak positively about him like "I bet your dad was happy to see you this weekend," or if they were talking about him, I'd join in and say, "Your dad sounds like he's pretty good at that. I know I couldn't do that." I didn't want it to be a competition. I wanted them to feel like they got the best of both worlds, not one world or the other. In a divorce, the kids have little to no control over their lives, so why shouldn't the parents work harder than they ever have before to give the kids more love, patience, and acceptance?

Ava

Ava is different. It took me quite a while to crack that nut. Both Ava and Bella watched my every move when I was around their mom. It was important for them to not so much hear about my affection for them and their mom. They needed to see it. And they need to continue to see it as our relationship evolves over time.

For Ava, I needed to demonstrate two things: (1) I'm no one to be afraid of, and (2) I care about you, your mom, and your sister.

Ava is the exact opposite of her sister when it comes to affection. She can't get enough of it. Imagine a little sugar monkey hanging off her mother from various angles as they walked through the jungle. She loves hugs, kisses, cuddles, and everything tactile. For some reason, she has always been intrigued by my bald head. Their name for me is Habibi. In many Arabic languages, that means "sweetheart." Jas came up with the name. Calling me by my first name always seemed disrespectful, and it would have set a bad precedent moving forward. Ava would always ask, "Habibi, can I touch your head?" Like a gentle Saint Bernard, I'd bend down so she could reach my head to give a few quick rubs on my shiny, smooth head to appease her curiosity. This would happen at least twice a week. I was happy to accommodate her request. She captivated my heart from the moment I saw her even though she was probably the most aloof toward me in the beginning. She was never rude, just distant (as to be expected). After making the request to touch my head about 122 times, okay, maybe not exactly 122, I told her that she didn't have to ask me, just go for it. It's like seeing that big Saint Bernard that used to seem intimidating, walk right up to you, and bend down for a head rub without any provocation. You've established a relationship.

If I had to guess what Ava's love languages are, I'd say physical touch and quality time. She loves for everyone to be together. I'm often required to have business dinners and travel, but I try to plan those around Ava's gymnastics practice as much as I can. I hate missing one of her practices, and I hate missing her meets even though I've had to because of that whole "integration is tough" thing I talked about earlier. It took a while for me and the girls' dad to be in the same place at the same time. For a while, we just observed our respective weekends and the activities that happen to fall on those days.

I remember once when Ava thought I was going to be at a work dinner, and I surprised her at the gymnastics facility. Her face lit up when she saw me. She wrapped her arms around me and clutched me tightly with her little chalk-covered hands. She was so surprised. When I told her that I try to plan my meetings around her practice schedule, she knew that I prioritized her. She knew that it was important for me to be wherever she was, encouraging her and being her big Saint Bernard in the corner, waiting for a head rub. I'm thankful for my relationship with Ava Bear.

Bryce

Bryce, my son, is at once uniquely fantastic and my greatest challenge. Don't get me wrong, as Curtis Jackson, a.k.a. 50 Cent, once said, "I love him like a fat kid loves cake," but that doesn't mean that he doesn't still drive me crazy from time to time. I've always said that children are a horrible ROI. They are a huge investment in time, money, and sweat equity, and they are a complete gamble in terms of their outcome as an adult. There are so many variables that can shift their lives in one way or the other. Imagine taking that time, energy, and money and focusing it on any other investment vehicle. The gains you'd get financially far outweigh the random tie, socks, or regifted Christmas gifts that children provide. Fortunately, I didn't choose to have Bryce for the financial return. As a matter of fact, I don't want a penny from my son. The greatest gift that he could ever give me is to become the man that he was created to be.

I was sitting in the parking lot of academy in August of 2011. I had just pulled into the parking spot, and for some strange reason, I felt an overwhelming presence. It was paralyzing, not in a physical sense but more in an emotional way. I didn't have the desire to move. I wanted to stay there, strapped in my seat belt, sitting in the parking lot with the engine still running and the air conditioner protecting me from the relentless Houston heat. As I sat there, I heard a divine voice. It was not in a spooky voice of Christmas past kind of way but more in a metaphysical, transcendent way that bypassed audible speech and went directly to mental comprehension. It was as if I'd heard the words clearly, without actually hearing them, and was comprehending what was just said.

You will have a son, and he will be a great leader. You will teach him to lead. I am developing you as a leader, not for yourself but for what you will teach your son who will be a greater leader than you.

Those words were as plain and understandable to me on that day as they are to you reading this book. Over the course of my life, I've had the ability to connect with God on various levels at various occasions. A year before my father died, I had a dream I was giving a speech in public and said, "My father died when I was sixteen years old." I was sixteen when he died from lymphoma. I gave a speech that included that line several years after his death. So needless to say, I had pretty high confidence that I would soon have a son. The leadership part was questionable, however. At that time, I was far from a leader. I was passive, unsure of myself, and scared to death to make a mistake, not exactly four-star general material.

In January of 2012, my ex-wife and I decided to visit an adoption agency to better understand the process. We just wanted to find out more information to decide if we wanted to go with this agency. I'd always wanted to adopt. My philosophy has always been that there are too many children in this world who have so little and were born into suboptimal circumstances. I wanted to adopt several children actually. Yep, me, Brad, and Angelina. I've always wanted to have children from all over the globe under the same roof. I'd been investigating various agencies from, literally, all over the world. I considered international adoptions, local adoptions, closed adoptions, and open adoptions. I'd talked to other adoptive parents before to find out their experiences and challenges.

Ultimately, I was convinced that an open adoption was the way to go. Open just means that the adoptive parents are aware of who the birth parents are and have limited access to the birth parents' medical and familial records. In some instances, birth parents have a degree of interaction with the child and the adoptive parents post adoption. It just made sense to me that if our kid ever had questions about his birth parents that we should have those answers available. Likewise, I wanted the birth parents to know that their biological kid was going to a great family. Before open adoptions were popularized, adoptions were these clandestine exchanges founded on privacy and discretion. Adopted children were forced to endure extraordinary measures to find any information about their birth parents. Questions often went unanswered, and multiple people, birth parents and children, were left unfulfilled and hollow because of a lack of awareness about each other. Prayers for the other fell on God's ears and remained sealed behind court orders and legal restrictions. I didn't want that for my child or for the birth parents who bravely gave their child to a stranger in hopes for a better life.

After listening to four hours of information and choking back tears from hearing adoption success stories, the orientation was over. As we were walking out, the director of the agency motioned for us to hang on for a second.

"Would you guys mind stepping in my office for a minute?"

I knew something was up. We hung out in her office as she escorted the other interested couples out. She came back in her office, closed the door, and then started to tell us how our lives were about to change forever.

"How do you feel about biracial children?"

Of course, we had no problem with biracial children. As long as the child was healthy, we would be fine. We knew that we just didn't have the capacity to care for a child with significant health or mental issues. God bless those who do. That just wasn't something that we were equipped to handle at the time although other people weren't necessarily ready to see me with a biracial kiddo.

"Your baby looks White." That was what one of my former coworkers said when she saw a picture of Bryce. She was a short, Vietnamese, thirty-something-year-old woman who had the tact of a ninety-year-old Black woman who just didn't give two nickels about anyone else's opinion. Apparently, when you get old, you gain the freedom to say just about anything and get away with it. I remember being at church and hearing old Black women talking about the attire of some of the younger ladies at church.

"Baby, Jesus don't need to see your underbritches and neither does Pastor Jenkins. Cover that shit up. Oh, Lord, forgive me for saying shit in the church."

My former coworker seems to have prematurely embraced her inner politically incorrect Black woman. I wasn't offended. I knew she wasn't trying to be malicious.

As soon as the adoption director asked us that question, I knew that she had a child in mind. She went on to tell us about a birth mom who was about to deliver in about nine weeks. Apparently, the birth mother was looking for an African American couple. She'd connected with one couple previously, but for some reason, she no longer wanted to match with them.

"How do you feel about a boy?"

My son, the son that God promised about five months earlier, was coming to fruition. I had no hesitation. I wanted to interrupt the director before she could even finish telling us about all that would have to transpire in order for the adoption to occur. Of course, I waited to consult with my ex.

Fast forward to integrating Bryce with Jas and the girls. Bryce has no filter. He's a kid, a rather creative kid. So while he has no filter and speaks in terms of great transparency, he also tends to embellish a bit just for the heck of it. The good thing is that Bryce fell in love with Ava and Bella at first sight. They started behaving like siblings, loving each other one minute and fighting with each other the next, sooner than we expected. The bad thing is that because Bryce was so excited about his new friends/bonus sisters, he would tell his mom all about his experience when he returned to her house. I never wanted to be hurtful to his mom, but her hearing the details of his weekends with me was, I'm sure, nothing short of tortuous. That wasn't my intent, but I couldn't tell Bryce to keep it a secret from his mom. I want him to be transparent, and I want him to be happy about sharing a life with me, Jas, and the girls.

I'm thankful for my relationship with my big guy, and I pray that I fulfill God's command to teach him to be the leader that he was born to be. I pray that we always have a great relationship.

Not Fully Anyone's Dad

There is a tremendous downside to this story of love and determination as we blend our families. Divorced dads, typically, bear a burden that leaves them feeling alienated from their own child and marginalized from their bonus kids. The divorced mom typically gets primary custody of the child. This also means that for all intents and purposes, she controls the flow of communication with the child if the child is not old enough to have his or her own cell phone. This is my case.

Despite any differences between the parents, I believe that we can all agree that for the benefit of the children, the goal should be to develop a working relationship that provides the children with the ability to have both a mother and father present in their lives to the extent that the parents are willing and able to be present. According to Dr. Douglas Darnall, there is a phenomenon that perpetuates distance from the noncustodial parent called parental alienation. The following are the signs or symptoms of parental alienation and are an indication that the parents are not successfully coparenting:

1. Giving children a choice about visits when there's no choice. Kids should be encouraged to spend time with each parent to continue progression of that relationship and to allow for the opportunity to answer questions that the child may have of each parent.
2. Telling the child *everything* about the previous marriage in the name of "being honest." Let's be real. There are some

things that kids just can't handle, and we, as adults, are responsible for bearing that burden. When the time is right, and in the appropriate context, anything can be divulged. Outside of those boundaries, we're just using the past as a weapon, and our children are the ones that are most deeply hurt. It's like aiming a gun at our ex and shooting our kids instead.

3. Refusing to be flexible with the visitation schedule and planning so many activities for the child that the targeted parent is not able to see the child. For lack of a better term, shit happens. Sometimes, dates may need to be switched so that life can be accommodated, and each parent can continue to nurture their relationship with the child and to provide some sense of continuity for both child and parent. By the way, filling the child's schedule from now until he's eighteen so that any request to be flexible is met with a response of "we have plans" is still parental alienation. It's no doubt passive-aggressive but still doesn't pass the test of a legitimate reason to deny flexibility. The requesting parent then becomes the villain and accused of not prioritizing time with his child. Again, attempts to hurt the ex impact the child by introducing opportunities for resentment, low self-esteem, and relational chasms. Other examples that Dr. Darnall provides include listening to phone conversations with the other parent, asking the child about the other parent's personal life, blaming the other parent for breaking up the family, etc. Some of these I've experienced personally, and some I have not.

I can tell you that the impacts of parental alienation hit their target, but they also cause unintended casualties.

An *International Journal of Adolescent Medicine and Health* article from 2015, titled "Parental Alienation: The Impact on Men's Health," indicates that male children are more highly impacted by parental alienation, not only as children but also as adult men.

Additionally, the fathers of children from whom they've been alienated may become depressed or suicidal.

I am, no doubt, crushed by being alienated, at times, from my son. Many nights, I've cried myself to sleep while holding one of his stuffed animals just to feel closer to him because I hadn't heard his voice in weeks or seen him in several weeks. Honestly, I don't care about that. I'm at least 50 percent responsible for not being with him, so I can deal with that. But let's examine the impact to the child. That same 2015 article and a 2013 *Psychology Today* article points to the serious consequences of parental alienation syndrome, which includes low self-esteem, self-hatred, lack of trust, depression, and substance abuse. Many children internalize their programmed hatred for the other parent and develop extreme guilt related to their feelings of betrayal toward the alienated parent. The articles go on to say that every child has a right to have a loving relationship with each parent, and denial of that right is tantamount to child abuse—child abuse.

Let that sink in for a minute. In some instances of parental alienation, a court-appointed intermediary was introduced to facilitate parental interactions. Clearly, this diminishes one's capacity to be a father.

With bonus kids, you get to be the "father figure" at times when the biological father isn't around. So 90 percent of the time, you get to feel like a dad, except for when it's a school function, a recital, or a competition. At best, you get to be the "other" dad or the mom's husband. You get to be close to being a dad but not so much. Yes, there is a tremendous amount of love and laughter from which you benefit that you wouldn't trade for the world. You may even have the benefit of providing guidance and perhaps even discipline. But you're always trumped by the biological. You're not the "real dad." That sucks.

The best thing that I've learned to do is to focus on those times that don't suck. I've learned so much from mindfulness practices that focus on being in the current moment. I enjoy the times that I am "dad" or "Habibi." I relish those moments, perhaps more now than I did when I was with my son 100 percent of the time, because I know they are fleeting. I don't always get to hear his voice. I don't always get to be Habibi when the girls are away with their dad. So I'll take every second I can get and store it in the recesses of my mind and heart to be recalled during those times when I'm feeling like a little bit less than a father. The reality is that parents don't always feel their impact on their kids. The day-to-day interaction really is just groundwork for the pivotal experiences. When the girls ask me cultural or political questions, I know that in that moment I'm helping to develop their worldview. That's dad work. When Bryce asks me questions about his anatomy as he gains awareness about his body and inquires about the differences in male and female anatomy, that's dad work. I thank God for those instances. They feed my hungry soul.

TREATMENT
[tret-ment]

Definition: The techniques or actions customarily applied in a specified situation

> *You treat a disease, you win, you lose. You treat a person, I guarantee you, you'll win, no matter what the outcome.*
>
> —Patch Adams

Growing up in church, having spent more Sundays than I can count listening to impassioned preachers, I've retained nuggets of previous sermons. I remember a pastor once saying, "Hate the sin, love the sinner." I know that sounds extremely churchy, but I agree with the sentiment. The way to treat the ills of any developed society is to understand and connect with the person behind the action. The challenge is separating action from person to be able to see the feasibility of an understanding.

CHAPTER 9

Racism Doesn't Have to Exist, But It Does

Social Experimentation

Today, diseases are fought through a number of sophisticated mechanisms that have been extensively tested for safety and efficacy. The beginning stages of the remedy, however, start with a theory followed by a testing of that theory. Cancer care is at a stage in its evolution where targeted therapy or immunotherapy is moving from the experimental to the standard of care. Targeted therapy basically looks at a person's unique molecular composition and the expression of certain hormones to determine what chemical agents will have the best chance at reacting with one's unique DNA to abate or eliminate the disease. It's even possible to proactively mitigate the chances of disease through genetic testing. Imagine a sixty-year-old woman enters an exam room for a mammogram. Based on a series of questions and an abnormal finding in her breast tissue, her medical provider offers information about genetic testing. The risk is that she's the carrier of a certain genetic mutation that predisposes her and her family members to breast cancer. After a brief consent and a sample, patients can discover the possibility of cancer in multiple generations and can begin to make a plan of care that will impact multiple family members. This is an amazing development in cancer care that began with one simple question. That question was, is there something within us that makes us more likely to have cancer?

I have a similar question as it relates to our eclectic society. Is there something within us that makes us more likely to bridge the chasms that are created through our respective life experiences? People have debated the nature versus nurture argument for years to discover the determining factor in human development, but I think it's safe to say that our environment plays a significant role in our worldview as adults. Lessons that I learned as a Black kid in urban Houston, Texas, are vastly different from a White kid who grew up in Upstate New York. Both of our experiences are different from a Jewish girl raised in Tel Aviv. Of course, they are. Why wouldn't they be? We didn't have the same challenges or the same advantages, so why would we learn the same lessons or be taught the same set of rules to live by? Even within racial or geographical subgroups, there's diversity of experiences based on individual family traditions and values. Each difference has the potential to create conflict with opposing views. History has demonstrated these conflicts by the existence of religious wars, hate crimes, interracial self-deprecation (i.e., marginalization based on skin tone seen in many racial groups), segregation, protests, and many other activities that illustrate the vast difference in perspective. The differences in development and cultural experiences inherently create chasms, but there's an intangible bridge that some people have the capacity to create and traverse while others don't. Do they ignore the differences of those they encounter to find the commonality among each other, or do they embrace those differences and seek greater understanding and appreciation for someone with different life experiences? What creates bonds between people that have very little in common that allows them to relate to each other and build significant relationships?

Attending a Vanguard High School in the middle of South Park (i.e., the hood) was a crazy experience. As I mentioned, a third of the school was populated by predominately Black kids in the "regular program." They had the typical high school curriculum, and my perception was that they also resented the other two-thirds of the school.

Perhaps I'm wrong, but random taunts of "fuck you, old uppity ass [N-word], you ain't special" gave me the subtle clue that there was some animosity brewing below the surface. The second group were the "pre-IB" kids. They took accelerated courses that helped prepare them for college. Again, these kids were predominately Black and still perceived to be more accepted than the third group. Finally, there were the kids in the "vanguard program," you know the "uppity ass [N-word]" kids. These were the nerds, and I was one of them. They also were the most diverse group in the school.

Kids came from all over Houston to be a part of this competitive program. It was a rigorous curriculum taught by teachers whose purpose was to help the kids excel on college entrance exams and to prepare them to be successful in college. A typical classroom was filled with students whose parents originated from Japan, Mexico, eastern Europe, Africa, Poland, and other assorted countries from around the globe. My best friend was a White kid, who grew up in the suburbs of Houston in a neighborhood that looked vastly different from mine. I remember visiting his house, and there was a pool in his backyard. All I had was a neighborhood pool that was often drained and used as a hangout spot for thugs and wannabe gangsters. We used to play ping-pong at his place on the weekends. His dad was cool, but his mom always looked at me like she thought I was going to take something. She probably took inventory before and after my visits. Despite feeling incredibly unwanted and undervalued by his mom, I never thought about ditching my best friend. I just thought his mom was an idiot, and I kept playing ping-pong.

My best friend and I hung out with a group of guys that made us look like a group of UN delegates. There was a Vietnamese kid, a Mexican, an Indian, and an Ethiopian. We never looked at our different cultures as a barrier. Actually, we used to laugh at our parents for what we thought were antiquated views. We'd make fun of, and validate, the random stereotypes and talk about how crazy they were. The Indian and the Vietnamese kids had to study like crazy and couldn't bring home anything less than an A. The Mexican kid's mom used to make him bring tamales to school and would threaten to throw her chancla at him if he misbehaved. The Ethiopian kid was really skinny and really good at long-distance running. We actually made fun of him the most. He was a good sport about it and took it on the chin a lot. He ended up becoming a nationally known physician, so I'd imagine that he has a pretty strong self-esteem these days.

As I look at that time in my life retrospectively, I can see clearly the social experimentation in which we were all engaged. In the clinical or scientific world, data is sometimes gathered without a defined study in mind. The rationale is that this information provides such diverse and rich details about a certain population of people that inevitably there will be a reason to study this group to draw conclusions about outcomes that transpire. Throughout the course of a research study, scientists often find that there is not one silver bullet that answers their questions or that causes that intended outcome. Rather, there are multiple elements that lead to the ultimate conclusion. Clinical trials often perform double-blind studies where one group is treated with the known standard of care and the other is treated with the standard of care plus the new drug or compound that's being tested for its efficacy. Ideally, this experimental combination will create either expedited or higher-quality outcomes than the normal standard of care.

As I think back to what held that group together and to what facilitated the deep relationships I've held with many other people of different ethnic groups since then, I have to believe that the compound that created that outcome is comprised of three elements. The first element is respect. I would argue that respect is the standard of care that we all need in any relationship. It's the "foundation" on which we build every other aspect. The second element is transparency. In order to fully understand someone, we have to be completely open in the communication of our thoughts and feelings to encourage meaningful discourse. The last element is grace.

Applying this three-layered compound somehow came naturally to me and to some of the people I've encountered in the past. I've never ignored cultural differences. They just didn't matter. If anything, the differences were intriguing to me. Stereotypes didn't dictate my actions. They gave me content for questions to ask in a transparent and inquisitive way. That inquisitive spirit was always bidirectional. I remember asking a Jewish friend about his beliefs about God and about that whole yarmulke thing. He didn't wear a yarmulke, but I felt comfortable asking him about it because I knew he wouldn't get offended. He'd asked me about Christianity and the messages of misogyny in some rap music. He even asked me why it seemed to be okay that Black people can use the N-word among themselves, but non-Black people couldn't use it. Despite the fact that I was taller than him and outweighed him by about sixty pounds, he felt safe to ask. He knew I wouldn't get offended. He knew that I would embrace that question as an opportunity to teach and to build our relationship even further. He knew that I would give him grace. We invested in each other by offering mutual respect, transparency, and grace to build a relationship that allows us to pick up where we left off at any point in the future even though he's a White guy from New York and I'm a Black guy from Texas. Chasms don't have to relegate us to being separate. We can see them as opportunities to build bridges that create a depth of relationship that strengthens the human experience.

Please Don't Be Black

The unfortunate element that often serves to exacerbate stereotypes and prohibits many from building bridges of understanding and unity is the media. My mom used to love to watch the news at least two times per day. At 6:00 p.m. and 10:00 p.m., I was forced to watch our local ABC news affiliate. For some reason, my mom was faithful to that news station even though they typically all reported on the same events. One of the local anchors, Dave Ward, was a staple of the news station during that time, and it just wasn't news if Dave wasn't saying it. Back then, we didn't have many stations, and the pliers that turned the broken knobs on the large, floor-model television were always near my mom or my dad, so it wasn't like I had a choice. All the cartoons had gone off by then, and they were mostly on Saturday mornings only anyway. Cartoon Network hadn't even been conceptualized when I was a kid, and the closest thing to

YouTube was watching my crazy neighbor across the street try to find her dog every night that kept mysteriously escaping. After all those repeated nights of walking down the street in hair rollers, slippers, and an unfortunately loose house robe, she really should have taken a hint. The dog just isn't that into you.

I hated watching the news. It was always the same thing. Someone got robbed, someone got shot, someone went to jail, and it just might rain tomorrow. All of those aspects of the news gave me great anxiety every day. I hated walking to or from the bus stop in the rain. Like many young Black boys, I didn't want to get my shoes messed up. I don't know what it is about Black guys and sneakers. My shoes weren't even Jordan's. My parents couldn't afford those. The best we could do was a solid pair of Reeboks or British Knights. Even more than rain, I dreaded hearing about violence or incarceration. It was as if I watched a lottery for my life every night. I remember hearing good old Dave talk about a random robbery or murder, and my first thought would be, "Please don't be in a Black neighborhood." Shortly thereafter, I'd hear Dave say, "It took place at the corner of Martin Luther King Boulevard and…." Damn. Okay, it's a Black neighborhood. My next thought would be, "Please don't let the bad guy be Black." "Eye witnesses report that the suspect was African American, between five foot eight and six feet tall, weighing between 180 and 220 pounds, last seen wearing blue jeans, a white T-shirt, and really clean sneakers." Damn. He's Black. Great, it was another vague description about a random Black man who committed a random act of violence. Were there no White people robbing or killing at that time? It seemed like every time I saw a Black face on TV, they were either playing professional sports or getting taken to prison.

Outside of the news outlets, there were movies and television shows that illustrated Black people in mostly negative, seldom positive, portrayals. I grew up watching shows like *Rock* and *Good Times*, which featured an all-Black cast but showed us as struggling individuals trying to make ends meet while leaning on each other as a family to survive. As a kid growing up in inner-city Houston, I wondered if this were art-imitating life or life being influenced by art. These shows certainly resonated with me as my childhood wasn't far removed from JJ and Michael Evans, but they gave me nothing to which I could aspire. Movies like *Roots*, *The Color Purple*, *Boyz n the Hood*, and many others were crucial to telling the story of the Black experience, but they weren't the entire Black experience. Don't get me wrong, these movies were major milestones in Black cinema, but we walk a dangerous line of imbalance when the majority of the images of Black people on the big screen illustrates a downtrodden people who often resort to cons, robbery, and violence to solve problems. It's not incorrect. It's incomplete.

For a very long time, we've been incomplete and imbalanced in the portrayals of African American images on the silver screen. I appreciate shows like *The Cosby Show* and *A Different World* that showed me that not only can we go to college, have fun, and get a great education, but we can aspire to be doctors and lawyers. We can be more than what we see in our immediate surroundings. This was a message similar to what my mom always told me. She said that with hard work, I could be anything, even the president of the United States, long before "Forty-Four" was even thinking about stepping into the White House. For some reason, despite what I saw walking to and from the bus stop every day, I believed her. I believed that I could do anything I set my mind to do. I just didn't know how to do it. I didn't have a road map to a positive future. I only had bread crumbs to a life of poverty and insufficiency. Those were scattered all around me. I needed more. I needed more examples outside of my home that could at least give me an idea of the direction I needed to take or even the possibilities of life in the future.

So if my internal monologue was wrestling with negative images of people who looked like me in the media, what impact must this have had on people who don't look like me? TV and movies are such powerful influencers and often help to shape our life perspectives. In a *Journalism and Mass Communication Quarterly* article in 1999 by Fujioka, he posits that people are influenced by positive or negative images of African Americans in the media especially in the absence of firsthand experience. A *Social Psychology Quarterly* article in 1997 by Ford demonstrated that negative images of Black people in the media strongly influenced not only White perspectives but also Black perspectives. I wonder if this explains all the times that people saw me walking down the street and immediately felt like the sidewalk was too crowded and moved to the other side. Or perhaps, it explains why female hands clutched purses a little more tightly or locked car doors as I moved in their direction. I've never robbed or beaten anyone, yet my appearance either led them to remember a previous negative encounter with someone who looked like me or led them to remember something they saw in the media. No, I'm not blaming the media for the struggles that are often levied upon us despite our status in life. I like the media in all its forms. I believe that the media is a powerful conduit that gives us crucial information about the world around us. It's not "fake news." It's just incomplete.

Post 9/11 America

I have to wonder that if it has been scientifically demonstrated that images on the TV and movies impact our perceptions, how does that impact perceptions of those in positions of authority? They are just as susceptible as we are to the negative perceptions. We know that racial profiling exists especially in a post-9/11 world. There were many Sikhs who were unjustly harassed by police officials in their communities and by TSA officials when traveling. Sikhs are not Muslims. In fact, their history indicates that they fought fiercely against an impending Muslim domination in northern India. According to American eyes, they just happen to have a similar appearance and wear similar traditional clothes. That's not true by the way. Muslims don't wear turbans. Unfortunately, most American's don't know that. Even if they were Muslim, should that have justified harassment? Should all our Muslim brothers and sisters be persecuted because a radical faction of their religion decided to wage Jihad against America? I get it. I was pissed too when I saw the twin towers collapse. I was devastated at the evil that hijacked planes, and I was emboldened by the people aboard flight 93 that caused the plane to go down in a field in Pennsylvania before it hit its intended target. But the moment we grab our pitchforks and torches and head out looking for random brown-skinned people in turbans and tunics, not only we demonstrate our susceptibility to images on television, but also we demonstrate how difficult it is to balance our emotions with reason to take steps to engage in discourse with those who are different or foreign.

In the days after the September 11 attacks, Balbir Singh Sodhi was murdered at his gas station in Arizona. Balbir was a Sikh who migrated to America from India in 1988. He came to this country in search of a better life, like many other immigrants, and began contributing to society by working at his brother's gas station. Balbir worked long hours, every day, to save money for his own business. Through conversations with many people who were not born in this country, I've learned that it is a common perception that they will have limited success working for American companies. They believe that their culture or their belief system or their style of dress will be rate-limiting factors in their ability to advance in corporate America. Therefore, in order to achieve the American dream of financial independence, many become entrepreneurs to take control of their financial fate. Some even feel as though they would not be able to be gainfully employed at all if it were not for a relative who had a business or for their ability to become entrepreneurs.

After having diligently saved enough money, he moved to Mesa, Arizona, where he opened his own gas station. Balbir was a husband and father of two daughters, who was tragically and senselessly murdered while working on his American dream. Frank Roque, who is now serving life in prison, murdered Balbir because he wanted to kill someone who he perceived looked like a terrorist. Having been angered by the brutal attacks on our country, like so many other Americans, Frank decided to take revenge on an innocent man who did nothing but wear a beard and a turban. Balbir wasn't the only person that Frank set his targets on. He went on to shoot other people who appeared to be of Middle Eastern descent.

The death of Balbir Sodhi is an illustration of the pervasive ignorance that infects our country. This fear of the foreign is what prohibits us from ever learning about the world around us. It is not pride in our country that keeps us from fully embracing the immigrant and the foreign. It is a fear that we will somehow dilute American culture. It is a fear that American citizens will be disadvantaged because of an increased population that will compete for limited jobs and opportunities. Pride is not the fuel that stokes the fire of those self-proclaimed patriots who protest and rally in the name of America. Fear is the culprit—fear of a future that is not dominated by the current prevailing majority and fear of a future that has an America filled with people of different religious beliefs, different tones of skin, and different languages spoken. "Sam" is afraid of an America that deviates from the look of our founding fathers. What Sam has yet to realize is that when we extend those rights and laws established by those white-haired White men a few centuries ago, we create an America that is better than ever imagined. Diversity is not America's enemy. It is its savior.

For years, I worked in corporate environments and have learned how to build successful organizations. It starts by creating an atmosphere of inclusion. Homogeneous thought, experiences, and beliefs lead to myopic outcomes. There is tremendous value in the debate that stems from differences of opinion and diversity of expertise.

One Wednesday evening, at about 6:00 p.m., I sat in a small auditorium as a surgical oncologist facilitated a planning conference to review the cases of several cancer patients with varying kinds of cancer. A radiologist ran the presentation and elaborated on the diagnostic images that were taken of each patient to provide expert content and commentary regarding the size and shape of the tumor as well as any metastasis. A pathologist was in the room as well to present the cellular behavior of the tumor and biological indications that would have a major impact on the proposed course of treatment. Medical oncologists debated the merits of certain prescribed courses of chemotherapy, stating newly published research that highlights new benefits and new toxicities. Radiation oncologists chimed in to suggest that risks could be significantly mitigated with minimal doses of high-level radiation. We reviewed about six cases that night, and each one was thoroughly discussed. Every physician in that room was integral to the conversation to make life-and-death decisions. If any one of those highly trained, highly subspecialized physicians are not represented, a patient will receive a less than comprehensive review and will suffer consequences that could at best lead to a poor quality of life and, at worst, death. Chemotherapy itself will not save a cancer patient especially if there has been no pathologist to determine the stage of the cancer or biological profile. No one kind of physician by him or herself can treat a cancer patient. No one kind of American can cure the ills and various prejudices of our society. People suffer when everyone shares the same thoughts, the same background, and the same experiences.

Do you get the picture? There's a reason why they say, "It takes a village to raise a child." It is not a White village or a Black village, but a village filled with a complex mix of backgrounds and experiences. Our country is greater because of the people who come to this country to make a better life. It is the metastatic behavior of people who would send us backward in time to the period shortly after the European invasion of the Native Americans and before the influx of immigrants, who came of their own free will, not those who were enslaved and stripped from their land. By the way, that's not immigration despite what some may call it to make the degradation of humans more benign in the history books.

We are strongest when we unite in our heterogeneity and in our common goal of making a great country collectively and a great life for our respective families and loved ones.

SURVIVOR

[sur-vi-vor]

Definition: 1. A person who survives, especially a person remaining alive after an event in which others have died

2. A person who copes well with difficulties in their life

> *You beat cancer by how you live, why you live and the manner in which you live.*
>
> —Stuart Scott

When the treatment is complete, whether or not it achieved its intended outcome, the person being treated must figure out the next phase of life. Based on the person's life journey, does he develop a new normal to continue living a fulfilling and meaningful life, or does he find peace and meaning with where he is, knowing that his old life is over?

CHAPTER 10

This Is Me. Love It or Leave It

I Love Me, Some Me

I've always been able to find the value in others to better understand and appreciate their perspective, but I've not always been so great at recognizing my own worth. My parents raised me to be a humble person. Unfortunately, I had a twisted perception of humility. I thought humility meant never accepting a compliment and never admitting to being the best. I remember excelling in school and being embarrassed about being number one. I didn't want the attention. I didn't want to be arrogant because to me, that's what arrogance was. My extreme humility devolved into self-deprecation. I began to limit my abilities as I looked at those around me. Instead of appreciating, and nurturing, the skills that God gave me, I focused on the skills of the people around me and how I couldn't do what they could do. I wasn't fast like that guy or tall like that guy. I wasn't as smart as that guy, or I couldn't sing like that person. I developed a laundry list of inadequacies that kept me sufficiently "humble."

In college, I remember going to step shows, waiting for the show to start so I could show the crowd how the ice-cold brothers of Alpha Phi Alpha "break stages." We were known for our apelike facial expressions, our hard and precise stepping, and our extreme bravado that oozed from our black and old-gold uniforms. We were cooler than the other side of the pillow, and we knew it. As soon as we walked in the auditorium, we let our swag swing from side to side with every step. We sat in a group together and chanted Alpha chants that had been passed down from generation to generation, modernized for the current era.

"A-L-P-H-A P-H-IIIIII, I'll be a badass Alpha till the day I die."

We didn't lack confidence at that time. As the other frats and sororities would perform before us, I remember waiting in the seat not being affected by their routines. I put my shades on, yes, in a dark auditorium at night, kicked my freshly shined combat boots up on the chair in front of me, and reclined in my swag. I would tell myself, *They ain't got nothing on you, Ice Cold. Wait until they watch you rock it, Ice Cold.* In hindsight, perhaps it sounds arrogant or, at minimum, corny. I accept that. But I had to do that. I had to pump myself up to combat the negative thoughts in my head. These days, they refer to what I was doing as repeating positive affirmations. At that time, I was just trying to provide an exceeding amount of confidence to battle the other voices that said, "What if you mess up? What if they laugh at you? What if you forget the routine? What if you slip or if you go left when you're supposed to go right or if someone heckles you?" There were so many negative thoughts racing through my head as a product of my insecurities and low self-esteem. The reality was that I was just a kid struggling for validation and appreciation. Like many at that stage of life, I was looking for a sense of belonging and purpose. The only way to get on stage and perform well enough to win was to build an extreme amount of confidence to overwhelm my insecurities.

Langston Hughes, in "Mother to Son," said, "Life for me ain't been no crystal stair." I can relate to that. But just because life has had thorns and cracks, that doesn't mean that I don't deserve love. I had to face some serious demons to reconcile with that statement. I deserve love. I deserve happiness. The only way to attain the love and happiness that I deserve, and for which I have been searching all my life, is to love myself. No, let me rephrase that. After my second divorce, I had to *love the hell out of myself.* In this case, the word *hell* is not used as a pedantic expletive. It's a placeholder for the hell that life can bring. I had to love the fear out of me. I had to love the self-deprecation out of me. I had to love out the guilt, the pain, the shame, the disappointments, the betrayal, the deceit, the unforgiveness, and the rejection from family and friends. I had to love the hell out of myself. I had to put on my shades, kick up my combat boots, and recline in overwhelming self-love and admiration to combat the pervasive negativity.

From a larger perspective, sometimes, the voices come from authorities much higher than you in a country that vows to protect and serve but never really defines who is included in that protection or service. It's implied that all Americans are afforded the same basic rights especially since passing the Civil Rights Act in 1964, but present-day and recent history provide little evidence of equality.

In recent data published by the United States Sentencing Commission, an independent agency of the United States Judicial Branch, it reported that African Americans were sentenced to prison sentences that were 20 percent longer than their White counterparts for similar offenses. Wrong is wrong, and I get that. I understand that every action has a consequence. However, how can we, as a people, feel that the laws of this country are intended to protect us when we are disproportionally punished? I could argue that the US judicial voice is screaming, "I don't want to protect you! I want protection from you! I don't serve you! I want you to remain in servitude by placing you at a disadvantage!" Given the various statistics of the probability of a Black man being incarcerated, I've had to ignore that voice all my life.

It's not easy to drown out the voices against you especially when some of them come from people who were closest to you. During the period shortly before my second divorce, I remember two of my best friends encouraging me to work things out with my ex-wife. They texted, called, and prayed. They tried everything I suppose they knew. What they didn't know is that I had access to correspondence between them and my ex.

"Take him for everything you can. He's like a robber. You don't want to shoot him, but if it comes between you and your son, then you have to do what you have to do." "My husband is so mad at him right now." My friends, whom I saw at their lowest points, point that I will not divulge ever despite the expiration of our friendship, saw fit to lay judgment upon, and, even more so, plotted to financially ruin me. I became their adversary. I was labeled a "robber," a criminal, someone who deserved to be imprisoned, and even "shot" (I think that was metaphorical). For months, I wore that label as if it were true. I deserved death. I was so depressed and emotionally despondent until I realized that being emotionally broken didn't benefit anyone, and it only served to destroy any future relationships that I hoped to have. It didn't benefit my son either, who needed a dad that would fight for him and fight to be with him. I knew he needed his dad to teach him things that only I could teach him, including learning from my mistakes of the past, all of them.

Mask Off

I know that I will have to be completely open with my son at some point about my past successes and lessons learned for his developmental benefit. On a recent trip to New Orleans, I got the inspiration I needed to understand how best to do that. New Orleans was an amazing experience filled with good food, interesting characters, and tales of resilience. According to our tour guide, the small city suffered two major fires in its three-hundred-year history. As we walked around, I couldn't help but notice the various people that populated the sticky, and sometimes offensively aromatic, streets of the French Quarter. There were those engaged in revelry and debauchery, seeking hedonism at all costs. There were those who asked for spare change for various reasons from "I just need weed money" to "fell on hard times." And then of course, there were the many talented singers and musicians who infuse New Orleans creativity and vitality into the atmosphere at almost every corner. I was fascinated as well by the elaborate Mardi Gras masks. Some of them were absolutely breathtaking.

It's amazing to think about some of the elaborate masks that we all wear every day. They cover our secrets, our insecurities, our fears, and our emotional wounds that we've yet to heal. They cover a myriad of things that we don't dare reveal to the world. The challenge is that when we wear masks every day, we lose who we are and never learn to appreciate to love ourselves.

I love listening to podcasts. I heard a guest on Shawn Stevenson's *Model Health Show* podcast that completely rocked my world. Her name was Lisa Nichols. One of the most poignant parts of her interview was when she said, "I've fallen in love with the darkest part of myself, and when you can fall in love with the darkest part of yourself…and bring him or her into every experience not wearing it, not putting it in front of you, but just, 'By the way.'" We have to remove our masks for our own emotional, physical, and spiritual health and for the health of others around us. If our scars can help heal someone else, then perhaps we should remove our decorative masks and reveal the truth of resilience and imperfection.

What we wrestle with as a society is the perfection paradigm, the thought that (1) I don't want people to know I'm not perfect, (2) other people believe I'm perfect, or (3) other people are perfect and I'm all wrong. We are all imperfect, but that doesn't diminish our value as human beings. It doesn't diminish our capability to contribute in a very meaningful way to society. I personally have had two failed marriages and made some very poor choices in my life, but I know I have much to give to the world despite the voices in my head that told me otherwise. They told me I was a failure and that I was undeserving of love yet a third time. They told me that I should give up and believe the lies that other people spewed about me behind my back. They told me that I deserved to be miserable for the rest of my life. I'll never forget that one person called me "the lowest piece of scum." It took me a while, but eventually, I wiped that comment from my soul as one would take a crisp white handkerchief and wipe one's cheek. That doesn't define me. It doesn't adhere to me. I won't allow it to do so.

So I remove my mask to reveal that truth of all my mistakes and all that I am. There's an expression that says, "Heavy is the head that wears the crown." I'd like to suggest that heavier is the head that wears the mask.

Cigars and Bourbon

One of my favorite pastimes is to sit peacefully with my thoughts, a glass of Belle Meade Bourbon with one large stone, and a 1964 Series Padron cigar. My preferred ritual is to lightly toast the cigar by exposing, but not touching, the cigar to the flame, allowing the end to evenly start to burn. I remove the cigar from the flame's heat, allow it time to breathe, and then expose it again while taking deep drags to ignite the end. Once lit, I take a final deep drag, holding the smoke on my tongue and then releasing it into the atmosphere as I hold the cigar in front of me to admire the wrapping and the perfectly even ash. One chasing sip of bourbon crowns the experience of the initial puff. I am unapologetically a fan of cigars and bourbon. I enjoy learning about different varieties of tobacco leaves and the aging and drying process. I frequently try new bourbons and occasionally find time to visit distilleries to take a tour and learn more about this spirited nectar. By now, I'm sure you get the picture that this activity gives me great pleasure. It's what I'd feel supremely comfortable doing if I were in a crowd of people or the only person in sight for miles.

One of my oldest friends has always been comfortable in his own skin. He had no problem being himself in the presence of princes or paupers. To him, they all put their pants on one leg at a time. We both pledged Alpha in college, so even though I've known him since he had a Jheri curl in middle school, we learned a lot more about each other later in life. Part of being in a fraternity meant supporting our other brothers. We had one brother who was a minister and was preaching at a church in Austin. He was a gifted speaker and was capable of captivating an audience from start to finish. As we sat in the pews listening to our brother preach, my oldest friend leaned over to me and said, "This muthafucker preaching, ain't he?" Did I mention that we were in a church? I've never seen God strike anyone down, but I figured that my boy was bound to at least get a little zap for that one. He has been a professional potty mouth for as long as I can remember, and the venue or audience has never been much of an influencer on his vocabulary.

As someone who has prided himself on being a chameleon based on the situation, I found this incredibly liberating and terrifying at the same time. I couldn't imagine just being myself regardless of the audience. I didn't even know what that looked like. I think at one point in life, I lost who I was, or never figured it out, and didn't know how to find myself. For years, I went through life with an identity crisis. I thought that the way to survive was to be who I needed to be when I needed to be that person. In middle school, I was teased in my neighborhood for being a nerd, so I downplayed my intelligence when I played basketball at the local park. When I went to school, it was assumed that since I was one of the Black kids that got bussed over from the poor side of town, I was dumb. So I went out of my way to demonstrate my intellectual prowess to prove them wrong. That ultimately evolved into adaptive behaviors as an adult. I had to keep my work friends separate from my nonwork friends because I was, almost literally, two different people. I'll never forget some years ago I tried out going by my middle name, Kyle, instead of my first name. I made a concerted effort to introduce myself as exclusively Kyle to a group of colleagues at work. For some reason, I ran into a group of my friends from college while at a work happy hour. I introduced them all and decided to let them mingle. Afterward, I went to the bar to get a drink, and as the bartender was handing me a glass, I turned to see my oldest friend talking to one of my colleagues. *Oh, shit,* I thought. You know that one friend that you know is going to keep it just a little bit too real? That's him. I tried to get to them as fast as possible to intervene and mediate the conversation, but I was too late. I heard my colleague ask, "So how do you know Kyle?" It was like one of those slow-motion movie moments where the hero dives in front of the bullet while screaming, "No!" Before I could get there, I heard my oldest friend say, "Who the fuck is Kyle? You mean Barrett?" And there went the short-lived exploration of going by my middle name.

Now that I'm older, I don't believe that life should be about pleasing other people or gaining their acceptance. I believe that life should be about becoming the absolute best version of who you are regardless of anyone else's opinion. When I adjusted my behavior to fit the occasion, I was just wearing another mask. I didn't allow anyone to get to know the real me because I didn't think the real me would be accepted. I couldn't take that. I couldn't risk someone not liking me. Yes, I know it sounds weak, but it's the truth. I'd rather some Bizarro version of me be rejected than the real me. That way, I could just create model 2.0 without the embarrassment of rejection.

I even played the role that I thought I was supposed to play with my family. There's a pretty large age gap between my siblings and me. My two older brothers are fourteen and fifteen years older than me, so I didn't really grow up with them. By the time I came along, they were busy teenagers who had one foot out the door, ready to jump into the real world. I loved, and even admired, my brothers, but we didn't know a lot about each other. My oldest brother loved motorcycles and was the first in our family to join the fire department. My other brother played high school football and became a minister pretty early in life. I was the shy, smart kid who did his best to stay out of trouble. My older sister, thirteen years older, was the peacemaker. That's the extent of our awareness of each other from my perspective. As long as we all stayed within those general parameters, the family dynamics remained in balance.

It wasn't until I became comfortable breaking that mold that my brothers and I gained a closer relationship. At every family gathering, after the dinner, the sports, and perhaps the gift exchange depending on the holiday, we retreat outside for a brotherhood smoke. Normally, we're at my oldest brother's house, so we go shopping in his humidor instead of bringing our own cigars. We each perform our respective smoking rituals to light the cigars and chase with a sip of our preferred bourbon to crown the experience. This is where we relax. This is where we shed our bravado and vent the emotional buildup that can only be released by cigar smoke and empty cocktail glasses. For years, I'd wanted a casual relationship with my brothers where I felt more like a brother and less like a son or a "baby brother." I maintained the behaviors I thought they wanted me to. I adapted to my siblings and kept playing the role of the baby brother instead of embracing who I am. The longer I held on to a persona, the more time I wasted that could have been spent getting to know my brothers.

I suspect the same is true in any relationship. Being our unique selves allows us the opportunity to purge those who can't accept the real you and attract those who can.

CHAPTER 11

My Therapy: Spirituality and Violence

Buddhism and Mindfulness

I saw a quote that read, "If you're depressed, you're living in the past. If you're anxious, you're living in the future. If you're at peace, you're living in the present." Like most people, I've always thought that "I'll have peace when" or "I would have peace if I would have." Never have I been very good at looking at the right now to find my peace. I almost feel like this is a conditioned phenomenon. For as long as I can remember, I've been waiting for something. I've been waiting for my parent's next paycheck so I could have that video game I wanted. I've been waiting until I turn driving age or drinking age to have fun. I've been waiting until I get that new job or that loan to start a business. It wasn't until recently that I noticed myself saying, "I'll be able to enjoy life once I retire." What the hell! I'm not even close to retirement age. Why would I prolong my happiness for twenty-five plus years? A better question is, how can I have happiness or peace now?

Remember the difference in the songs sang at predominantly Black churches versus those sang at predominantly White churches? The White churches would sing about how great and mighty God is. Of course, it would be sung in a very reserved and professional fashion. The congregation would sway from side to side uniformly as blades of grass sway in sync in the wind. It would be beautiful. The following sermon would be preached by a straitlaced Southern Baptist preacher with great eloquence, speaking of a triumphant Jesus.

Black churches would have some of the most passionate and talented singers I've ever heard in my life. The octave ranges of some of these gifted people would be absolutely mind-blowing. I swear Sister Jenkins put a crack in the stained glass window when she hit that high note in her rendition of "Take Me to the Water." The choir director would "catch the spirit" at least twice and would call each section of soprano, alto, tenor, and baritone individually to spotlight their voices. Then he'd take out a perfectly placed pocket square, pat his brow three times, and then bring the sections together in precise harmony to fill the church walls with a beautifully thunderous choir that made angels themselves smile. People would be dancing in the aisles, unable to be contained in the pews.

The other noticeable contrast was the perspective of the culture of the church. Maybe it was just my church, but it seemed like all the songs and sermons pointed to some point in the future. We'd talk about "making it through the storm," "trouble not lasting always," and "we shall overcome." I can appreciate the struggle especially given that most of the churches I attended were in lower socioeconomic neighborhoods, but the contrast was undeniable. It was as if the Black churches were searching for a peace that the White churches had already attained. I think there are many variables that account for my perceived contrast, but my purpose is not to debate the differences in the two cultures. It's to highlight my experience of being conditioned to believe that peace is a perpetual future state. I learned to believe that peace was circumstantial and reserved for only certain people to experience now. Everyone else would have to wait until later.

Most of us believe that we'll have peace when we get that promotion, that house, our health gets better, or when we hit the lottery. Some of us believe that peace evades us because of mistakes or missteps of the past. If we would have only made better choices about our profession, or about our partner, or perhaps if we would have selected a house in a different neighborhood, then we could have peace now. But since that didn't happen, peace remains elusive. I would argue that a relative minority of people have the ability to recognize peace when they see it. Oftentimes, there are too many distractions that prevent us from seeing peace. It's like peace is Waldo, and it's surrounded by a cluster of bills, heartache, desire, ambition, failure, self-deprecation, etc.

I've always been fascinated by Buddhist philosophy, but I began to adopt some of the Buddhist practices in an attempt to find Waldo today, not tomorrow when circumstances become ideal. The four noble truths of Buddhism are as follows: (1) Suffering is an inevitable part of life; (2) suffering is due to our desires; (3) suffering is avoidable, and peace is possible if we relinquish those desires; and (4) the eightfold path is the way to attain peace and avoid suffering.

No, I don't go around wearing a maroon bedsheet, chanting Tibetan hymns, nor do I sit in lotus position for hours waiting for nirvana. I do, however, accept the concepts of the four noble truths:

1. Life sucks at times. This is indisputable I believe. Perspectives dictate that my version of sucking may be different from others, but as Shakespeare once said, "Sucking by any other name still sucks the same." Okay, that was Leroy Shakespeare, not William. It's funny listening to what people classify as a bad day. For some people, a bad day means that a bird dropped a bomb on their recently washed Range Rover, and they don't have time to wash it before they go to the annual holiday gala. Yeah, that sucks. For some people, a bad day is getting splashed by some creep that hit a puddle at the exact time you happened to be walking on that section of sidewalk as you're headed to the bus stop, trying to make your way to a job interview for a second job because you can't make ends meet for you and your family with just one job. Yeah, that sucks too.

Whatever our station in life, we all have a perspective of suffering.

Accepting the fact that as long as we're alive, there will be suffering helps to at least set our expectations. We know that things won't be perfect, so we shouldn't expect perfection. We can be prepared and expect that bird poop, that jerk in the black Honda CR-Z who can't drive around puddles, that missed promotion, that failed marriage, and that unexpected death. I'm sorry there is pain in this world. I'm sorry that life sucks sometimes. There may be times where life may even seem suicidal, but if we set our expectations with the understanding that because suffering is inevitable, we should thank our Creator for every second of joy. Not only should we be thankful, we should relish in it. We should behave as though the happiness we're experiencing at that moment is a huge pile of whatever you want it to be (money, leaves, snow, cotton candy, whatever), and you're playing in it like a child. Laugh hysterically, hold your loved ones so tight you make it slightly hard for them to breathe, and kiss your significant other as if you haven't seen her for years. Really embrace those moments with every sense that you have. Smell the air as you watch your son run and play at the park. Feel the warmth of the sun on your skin as you sit at the beach with your husband. Notice the rhythm of your heartbeat and the sense of pride you feel as you watch your daughter's performance. Feel it! Don't take a second of peace for granted.

2. We suffer because we want stuff. For some of us, we just like to keep up with the Joneses. We want the latest model luxury car, we want the most fashionable clothes, we want to take the most lavish vacations, and we want to send our kids to the best schools. None of this is necessarily bad, but it creates expectations, and if we're not careful, it creates entitlements. As a society, we are entitled to life, liberty, and the pursuit of happiness. We are not entitled to have every single thing our heart desires. I believe in aspirations,

goals, dreams, desires, etc. I also believe in working my ass off to get what I want. I do not believe in the concept of acquiring things just because I woke up this morning, because I was born into a certain family, or because I just feel that I deserve whatever I want. The fact of the matter is we suffer when we want stuff that we don't have or don't get. Sometimes, that suffering drives our ambition and serves as motivation to work hard to achieve our goals. Other times, what we want may be unattainable or at least not quickly attainable. I remember watching a beautifully talented young woman who was constantly looking around her at what everyone else had or could do. Her narrative was, constantly, "I wish I had what they had," "I can't do that like they can," or "it's not fair that they have that. I want that too." What she neglected to embrace was the fact that she has a brilliant mind that's capable of just about anything. She is effortlessly graceful and highly creative. She has an affinity for drama, dance, and singing, and if she nurtured those God-given gifts just a little bit, she could blossom into a talented artist.

Sometimes, we suffer because we spend too much time looking out of the window instead of looking at the mirror. Trust me, there is something beautiful about all of us. There is something unique and special within each of us that if we embraced and nurtured those God-given gifts just a little bit, we could not only abate our own suffering. We could abate the suffering of our communities around us. How many times have we said, "I can't help them right now. I need to help myself." Okay, I feel you. But are we helping ourselves? Are we doing something to move the needle toward improvement so that we can help others? When we stop judging ourselves by what we don't have instead of valuing ourselves for what we do have, we can begin to accept the jewels that we are and can help others see their worth as well. It's okay to want stuff, but we have to remember to take a second to look at all that we have and all that we are before we get overwhelmed by all that we want.

3. Stop wanting stuff, and you'll stop suffering. What I mean by "wanting" is different than you may think. I'm not implying that we should become ascetics and give away everything that we own, left to wander about life aimlessly. There's another Buddhist concept called attachment. We become so attached to things, and people, that sometimes we begin to idolize and deify them. We cling tightly to either the desire of something or someone or to the actual existence of that thing that if we ever lose that thing that we will be devastated. This is why we're so impacted when we don't get that promotion, that home loan, or when that big business deal collapses at the last moment. This is also why divorce or loss of love is so hurtful. Parents cry uncontrollably when their kids go off to college. I'm sure I'll experience that as well when my oldest bonus daughter goes to school in a few years. It happens. The way to manage this, however, is to be able to fully love and enjoy something or someone and be able to let go when it's time to do so.

Throughout my life, I've kept people at arm's length. I rarely allowed close relationships and intentionally kept my circle of friends very small. I never allowed myself to get excited about getting things or traveling to cool places. I tried to stay level. I figured that if I didn't get too excited about something that I couldn't get disappointed if that something didn't manifest. I kept most relationships at a distance because I didn't want to deal with maintaining the relationship to keep it going, ultimately to avoid it from demise. This was an incorrect way to avoid getting too "attached" to someone or something. That Buddhist concept of attachment is not implying that we should not allow close bonds and lack desire for things. The implication is that regardless of the depth of the wanting that we must be able to let go if we need to. Sometimes, relationships end or evolve, for whatever reason, and we have to be able to recognize the evolution and be thankful for the time we had with that person. Hopefully, we took time to appreciate the good moments when they happened. Hopefully, we loved deeply and fully. Hopefully, we learned and grew from that relationship. However, holding on to someone with a white-knuckle grip, kicking and screaming as life is taking you and/or this person in a different direction, is not helpful or healthy. Let go. Life has a different path now, and peace awaits in a different direction.

4. There is a path to follow to have peace. The eightfold path is a specific set of guidelines for living that all point to increasing our moral compasses and strengthening our thirst for knowledge and compassion for others. The moral of the story is that we can have peace now, and it's not based on what we have or what we're able to do. It's based on our intrinsic ability to silence the noise and focus on the gifts that God has already given us.

I like to meditate outside. I've always felt especially close to God in nature and now find it incredibly peaceful to sit among God's creation to hear moving water and to feel the breeze as I quiet the noise in my mind and open my soul to the light and energy of God. The light is the truth of God that overrides every negative self-image or derogatory comment uttered, or even thought, by someone else. Haters may not always say what's on their minds to maintain their anonymity, but God protects us from them as well. The energy is the will and plan for our lives that God designed before time began, and that cannot be obstructed my any man or woman. When we connect to God and walk in the path that He's laid before us, there is no force that can change what God has planned for us. I want to give all of my kids a life more amazing than they could ever imagine. I want to show them the world and give them every advantage to be successful in life. I want to give them so many smiles that they develop laugh lines because their lives are filled with so much freaking joy. I want to love the hell out of them! If I, as an imperfect and highly flawed being, have this desire to give my kids happiness, how much more must an omnipotent Creator desire to give His creations more happiness than we can contain?

Krav Maga

In the 1930s, a guy by the name of Imi Lichtenfeld developed a fighting style that would later be the hallmark of the Israeli military. This fighting style, Krav Maga, was later adapted for civilian self-defense and is based on a few key principles:

1. Weight transfer. One of the drills that we do at Krav Maga Houston, not sure if it's the same in other locations, is called boogie the line. For most beginners, myself included, the first time is rather demoralizing. The idea is to be able to advance forward while throwing punches by transferring your weight from left to right. It sounds easy, but the first time you boogie the line, you look more David Hasselhoff during his brief stint on *Dancing with the Stars* than Sylvester Stallone in *Rocky*. It's clumsy, uncoordinated, and frustrating. It's also not the most fun exercise. Most people come to Krav because they want to kick some ass, not learn how to move gracefully from side to side. However, any good student understands that we can't even begin to talk about advanced fighting techniques if we don't have solid fundamentals. It's like any sport or activity. There must be a strong appreciation and a solid understanding for the basic elements to develop complex skills. The other reason that necessitates a good understanding for how to transfer weight is the principle of being able to focus every ounce of power in your body to the weapon you're using. For example, when throwing a punch, the idea is to make every punch count. Ideally, you throw one punch and get to go home safely because your attacker is on the ground seeing

stars. Most likely, it will take more than one punch. It will take many. But in order to make this fighting style effective for people of all sizes, ages, and genders, the student must focus all of his or her energy on that fist traveling toward the attacker's face. The entire body must move in a way to maximize the power in that one fist. A strong side punch requires that the lead foot be planted firmly in front and the back heel slightly elevated and ready to be driven into the ground as if to put out a cigarette. The strong side hip and shoulder must thrust forward, supporting the force of the fist, effectively transferring the body weight from strong side to weak side or right to left for most people. A punch is not just a single fist traveling haphazardly toward an attacker. It is a coordinated strike with your entire body using the fist as the tip of the execution point.

2. Go into the fight. At the beginning of most classes, after rigorous calisthenics and shadowboxing drills to warm up, the instructor yells, "Fighting stance!" Instinctively, we respond by aggressively taking a step forward, tucking our elbows to our sides, and raising our fists to about chin level prepared to respond to a threat. Every combative that we're taught follows the same theme. Move forward. Don't run away from the fight. Run into it. Each technique teaches us to address the bodily threat by either blocking a strike or breaking a choke hold and then simultaneously counterattacking by taking the fight to the attacker. I love the way one of the coaches phrased it. "I didn't plan on a fight today, but fuck it. We're here now, so let's go!"

3. Speed and leverage. Let's face it. There will always be someone bigger, stronger, or faster. The way to go home safely is to not get into a battle of strength with someone. Technique will beat strength nine out of ten times. I like finding the biggest guy in the room to partner with. One reason is because I like being forced to use speed and leverage instead of strength. The other is because I like knowing that I can affect someone bigger than me. There's a basic

technique used when an attacker is choking you called the pluck. The idea is to use the speed of your hands and the leverage of your body to break the choke. The pluck is only effective if done fast. Anyone that decides they are going to choke you assumes that he's stronger than you and just that pissed off that he wants to watch your facial expressions as you gasp for air. Grabbing their arms or wrists and trying to wrestle with them are only going to piss them off even more. Plus, you give them the opportunity to think about a different attack. Quickly plucking their choke and sending a quick foot to the groin or palm-heel to the chin will be much more effective. After the initial counterstrike, refer to principle number two.

4. Flip a switch, and go apeshit. When we train, we train with men and women with whom we've built a relationship. These people are lawyers, doctors, commercial realtors, law enforcement officers, entrepreneurs, baristas, tattoo artists, stay-at-home moms, etc. They come from all walks of life. None of us has any desire to injure our training partner. However, we have to train as if our partner, Johnny Project Manager, is a bad guy. We have to learn that in the real world, an attacker is not going to pull punches and go easy on us. Anyone who attacks us or our families intends to severely impact our quality of life, if not kill us. We have to know how to flip a switch in our brains and go absolutely ballistic as we apply learned techniques to break someone's face, crack their rib cage, or put your elbow through their eye socket, among other creative combative attacks. When the choice is you and/or your family going home safely or watching someone you love breathe their last breath because some guy decided to attack you, you summon the animal within you, and you unleash a furious rage to protect that which you hold dear.

Krav has taught me much more than just how to disarm a guy with a weapon or knock a guy out with one punch. As I reflect on what I've learned from others, I realize that these four principles lead to success:

1. Weight transfer or focused effort. For as long as I can remember, my mom has always told me that "I can do anything I put my mind to." The ability for a person to quiet the noise in his or her brain and just focus all energies toward accomplishing that one thing is a key element to success. I think back to when I've prepared for a test in school or prepped for a big presentation at work. I couldn't allow myself to be distracted, and I couldn't exert a half-hearted effort. I had to give everything I had to that one particular task, using all of my collective energy to support my efforts. The tricky part for me has always been to pivot and shift that energy to another task, then another task, and then another task. In life, there is a constant shifting of "weight" to pivot to the next challenge, to address it, and to attack it. Success happens when we're able to focus everything we have on accomplishing a particular task and then shifting our weight to respond to life's next opportunity.

2. Go into the fight or never stop progressing. I've not met many people who have had an easy life. That's just not my circle. I've been around people who have struggled through adversity to become who they are today. I've known people who have been divorced multiple times and who now are in happy and successful marriages. I've known people laid off from jobs who now are either executives in multinational organizations or wildly successful entrepreneurs. Sometimes, there are things in life that are holding us back from being the best possible versions of ourselves, and we have to be bold enough to make some big, tough, scary decisions that will make those who love you most scream in horror as they watch you "wreck your life." You may have heard of a guy that started this small computer company while he was in college. We actually both grew up in Houston, and we both attended the University of Texas at

Austin. He only completed one semester there. His parents were mortified when he told them he planned to drop out. Fortunately, he's doing okay now. He's worth over $20 billion, employs thousands of people, gives away millions of dollars in philanthropy each year, and lives in a beautiful house in Austin, overlooking the school that would have just held him back had he decided to remain there as a pre-med student. Not everyone will become Michael Dell, but we can choose to do things in life that keep us moving forward regardless of what other people may think, regardless if no one has ever done it before, and regardless if we've had a rough life so far. There are too many examples of people who have come from next to nothing and who have been able to pull themselves up and make something beautiful from ashes and rubble. Our biggest obstacle is often the person we see in the mirror every day. Regardless of what has happened or where we are in life, we can all choose to say, "I didn't plan on being here, but fuck it. I'm here now, so let's go!"

3. Speed and leverage or timing and positioning. I've heard it said that success happens at the intersection of opportunity and preparation. We have to be in the right place at the right time and ready to capitalize on the moment. Years ago, I had an idea to make a pilot that featured local Houston restaurants. I did the groundwork to find the business owners, contact them, and obtain appropriate approvals to film and everything else involved in producing a very small-scale pilot. During the course of that filming, I met the principal investor of one of the restaurants. We had a brief conversation and hit it off well. He asked what my future plans were, and I pitched him other ideas I had for television productions. Ironically, he also owned a minor league baseball team. As a result of that opportune meeting, I was able to gain access to the team, the players, the stadium, etc. I filmed the team and spent the day with leadership from the Round Rock Express. I was prepared

to take advantage of a chance meeting and had an opportunity to continue my short-lived career in television production. It was short-lived because I didn't follow principles one and two after this day of filming. There was a problem with my equipment. All footage, every single second, was lost. It was a wasted day and a wasted opportunity. I have no idea what happened, but what I do know is that I let that experience stop my progress. I didn't shift my weight to try to pivot to another opportunity, and I didn't keep progressing in spite of this major setback. I quit. That was a huge mistake and a lesson I'll never forget. You may know this, but the Round Rock Express is a feeder team for the Houston Astros. You know, the World Series Champion Houston Astros. Who knows what kind of access or connections I would have had today if things had worked out differently or if I would have made the choice to go into the fight?

4. Flip a switch, and go apeshit or relentlessly pursue your dreams as if your life depended on it. Great change is not possible without great effort and great sacrifice. Many of the people I've studied over the years have become successful only through herculean efforts and dogged pursuit of their goals. I can't speak for everyone else's experience, but my parents taught me that life is not easy for someone who looks like me and who grew up in the neighborhood that I did. So my ticket out would have to be hard work. "You have to work twice as hard as the White kids do to prove your worth." I remember hearing this when I was in elementary. As racially charged and stereotypical as it may sound, this was my parents' reality. They grew up in a time where "Colored people" were treated like animals instead of equals. My mom told me stories of when she was forced to use the "Colored drinking fountain" and had to go in through the "Colored entrance" (i.e., back door) of public establishments. There were no caveats for a person's character or personality. The color of your skin was the only

measure by which a person was judged. So even though the "Whites only" signs had been removed from buildings when I was growing up, my parents were still astute enough to know that those signs still hung in the minds of many in our society.

So that's what I did. I developed a ferocious work ethic that ultimately led me through many sleepless nights studying for exams and sitting on the floor in my room working on math problems until I was blue in the face. I didn't want to let anything beat me, and I didn't believe in excuses. That doesn't translate to everything in my life. I'm not perfect, but in some areas, there was nothing that was going to stop me from reaching my goal.

I grew up a chubby kid and was always just one burger away from being full-blown fat. Honestly, as I look back at some of my postcollege pictures, I was definitely a full-blown fat at least for periods of my lifetime. I was tired of the yo-yo weight gain, weight loss that I seemed to be prone to experiencing. I wanted to really dial it in and try to get in my best shape. I knew how to work out due to my brief stint as a collegiate powerlifter and my personal training business that I'd had years ago. I knew what to do. I just needed the motivation and stubbornness to carry through with it. I decided to enlist the help of one of the hundreds of workout programs that you pop into your DVD player and follow for thirty, sixty, or ninety days. If the only time I had to work out was 4:00 a.m., then I worked out at 4:00 a.m. If I hadn't worked out all day and needed to stay on schedule, then I'd workout after everyone had gone to sleep and my responsibilities to everyone else were complete even if that was not until 12:00 a.m. It didn't matter. I changed my eating habits tremendously. I was regimented, calculated, and focused on macro-nutrient intake, not flavor. Yes, you can have both, but that didn't matter to me. I was determined to get in the best shape of my life. I was belligerent about fitness, and as a result, I lost over thirty-five pounds in three months, dropping a significant amount of body fat and wearing clothes sizes that I hadn't worn in years. Everyone has the ability to be laser focused on something even if its laser focused on a bad habit. The challenge is translating that focus to something that's meaningful and constructive.

I'm at a stage where my life does indeed depend on pursuing my passions. I will, quite literally, die an early death if I don't do what I love. I need to tell stories that move people through thought-provoking literature, media, and talks. I need to impact our future by reaching and helping our children who are entangled in societal ills like obesity and sex trafficking. I need to empower others by creating jobs that feed our communities. For so long, I've felt like a man wearing an ill-fitted suit. Though I have achieved a measure of success professionally, my life has not been the life I was born to live, and I refuse to live another second in mediocrity. I will fight with all that I have to become the man that I was born to be. I have flipped a switch in my brain that compels me to fight with all that I have until all my goals are realized, and I will not back down. I will shift my weight, go into the fight using speed, and leverage going apeshit on any obstacle that comes between me and the life and legacy that I want for my family.

CHAPTER 12

Stage 4 Urgency

Stage 4 Urgency

I once had the privilege of interviewing an aspiring breast surgeon. She was just finishing her fellowship at Northwestern University at Chicago. Her CV was fairly impressive although it's difficult to accurately depict the numerous and varied experiences of a clinical surgeon. What was most impressive about her was not listed on paper. It was what her character displayed during our conversation. She was a young woman, most likely in her late twenties, who was impeccably dressed. Her Muslim heritage was proudly on display as she wore a fashionable hijab that matched her couture black-and-white, polka-dot suit. She told me that she was originally from Iraq and was taken as a prisoner of war during the Gulf War. As she told her story, her expression was not one of anger or sorrow. It was as if this tragic event were a footnote in her life. She recounted the story in such a nonchalant manner as if she were saying it as a part of a bigger climax to the story, and this was only a crescendo. There were times in the POW camp that she feared for her life and the lives of her family members and loved ones.

"If you asked for more food, they'd shoot you. If you asked for more water, they'd shoot you. If they just didn't like you or the way you looked, they'd shoot you."

As a young, five-year-old girl, she'd walk around with the imminent fear of death, not knowing if she'd do something that provoked a soldier's trigger finger.

Eventually, she was able to leave the camp and came to America. She decided to study medicine and wanted to be a general surgeon. This young woman was all too familiar with death and decided that she'd become someone who could help to prevent it. During the course of her training, she was able to return to Iraq after not having been there since she was a POW. It was a surreal experience for her. This was ground that her feet had not touched since she was severely oppressed and relegated to the life of a criminal. She met countless patients who severely needed her help. One woman she encountered was bleeding from her eye. The woman had been sick for quite some time yet went undiagnosed. After an examination by this aspiring surgeon, it was discovered that this woman had metastatic breast cancer so severely that tumors had spread throughout her body and was literally coming out of her eye. This was one of the worst cases of breast cancer that she'd ever seen. It was so pivotal in her life that she decided to devote her career to becoming a breast surgeon. She left that experience with such a sense of urgency to help women around the world. This poor woman ignited a passion within the surgeon that would fuel her career and inspire others who would hear that story.

The severity of cancer is based on stages. Stage 1 cancer is the lowest grade with stage 4 being the most severe. The goal, of course, is to detect cancer as early as possible. That's when the most treatment options are available. There are many things that can be done preventatively, of course, but where prevention was omitted, early detection is the next best scenario. As the cancer progresses in stage, the treatment options begin to diminish, and the sense of desperation and urgency begins to rise. Stage 4 cancer introduces experimental treatments and conversations of hospice and palliative care. It's not necessarily a death sentence, however. As a matter of fact, I know many stage 4 cases that turned out to have very positive outcomes where the patients have gone on to live long lives posttreatment. It doesn't have to end in death, but the treatment has to be aggressive, and the patients and caregivers must have a sense of urgency.

We are at a point in American history, although some would argue that we've been here for a while, that we need to have a stage 4 sense of urgency.

When Trayvon Martin was killed in February of 2012, it felt like there was a tumor that was found in "Uncle Sam" that if left unchecked would spread. Make no mistake, we've had tumors, infections, bleeding, and general sickness in America for years. This was just one more of many preexisting diseases. On one side of the conversation, there were those who cried injustice for the killing of an unarmed Black teenager. The other side were those who believed that George Zimmerman was justified and, just like everyone else, has the legal right to bear arms and protect himself if he felt that his life was threatened. This tumor was indeed left unchecked, and as predicted, it spread across our nation, creating divides in numerous communities between various classes of people.

We witnessed an epidemic of police-related murders that stoked the fires of injustice and gave more relevance to community activists and political groups who worked to fight inequality and racism. Black Lives Matter became the antithesis of Blue Lives Matter, unintentionally creating more of a divide than serving as a demonstration of the importance of all humanity. As an American citizen, I've always had a healthy respect for law enforcement. As a Black man, I've always had a subterranean fear of the police. They are charged with protecting and serving the communities in which they work, but that's unfortunately not been a consistent experience. No one is perfect, and I understand well that their lives are on the line every time they walk out the door, but who can justify a policy officer driving his knee into George Floyd's neck, using his full body weight, for eight minutes and forty-six seconds? Who can explain how Breonna Taylor can get killed in her own home by police officers purportedly executing a no-knock warrant when her only offense was sleeping while Black?

When Eric Garner was killed in July 2014 after screaming that he couldn't breathe after being put in an illegal choke hold by law enforcement in New York, I thought it was a horrible event that went way too far. When an eighteen-year-old Michael Brown was killed in Ferguson in August of 2014, I was enraged and left feeling that people who looked like me were insignificant in the eyes of the law. When a twelve-year-old Tamir Rice was killed in November of 2014 in Cleveland, my heart broke. He reminded me of my own son, and he reminded me of the lens through which Black men are seen. It's as if there's a set of "Black-noculars" that distort their view to show an image of evil. A hoodie on a Black man means that he has bad intentions, but on others, it just means they're cold. A toy gun in the hands of a young Black boy is a lethal weapon, but a real gun in the hands of second amendment enthusiasts is a constitutional right. With fear and disdain in my heart, I reflected on these and many other men who have had their lives cut short by the hand of injustice, and I thought to myself, *Oh my god, this is starting to spread.*

The spread of racism, sexism, bigotry, hate, and inequality in any and all forms is not a new phenomenon. It is passed down like a toxic heirloom that serves to reincarnate the hate from the generation before. Like crops that are not yet ready for harvesting that are ravaged with pestilence, so do our children become tainted by residual prejudice and present-day manifestations of fear and hate for that which is different or foreign. We must stave off this metastatic behavior. We can stop this if we aggressively work to illuminate our differences in a constructive manner, seeking to first understand each other. With a foundational understanding that we are all someone's relative, someone's lover, someone's friend, and someone who matters to someone else, we can begin the conversation of creating communities that nurture those relationships and selflessly serve the needs of the people. I'm not talking about utopia. I'm talking about taking a second to see and hear each other. Take a moment to see past the hurt that often begets more hurt. Take a moment to listen past the vitriol and hear the fear. Take a moment to appreciate the glimpses of compassion between God's creations.

We are a resilient nation, and while the prognosis may be bleak, we can recover. We can shed light on sexual abuse and give voice to those who have been shamed into silence for far too long. When

Tarana Burke created the phrase "me too" in 2006, she had no idea that Alyssa Milano would take it viral on Twitter in October of 2017. Burke's phrase became a popular hashtag that would spread world-wide and become the banner for women who were taken advantage of by men whom they trusted with some aspect of their career. Especially close to my heart are the young women who were victimized by Larry Nassar. I see Ava in the eyes of the Nassar's victims, who bravely came forward to testify of the horror they experienced under his care.

Of the over 260 girls that he sexually abused, one father tried to attack Nassar in court after hearing his daughter's testimony. I wasn't mad at him. I'd do the same thing. It would be my distinct pleasure to cause extended and insatiable pain to the person that hurts any of my kids. However, #metoo was just the beginning. It gave way to introduce #timesup, the movement that would further empower women to raise their voices against unwanted sexual advances and sexual offenses. At the 2018 Golden Globes, Ms. Oprah Winfrey gave a moving speech that prompted rumors and whispers of a presidential run in the next election. Ms. Winfrey, can I talk to you for a second? I love you, Oprah, but I don't want you to be my president. I want you to be the charismatic and independent woman who you are. Only in your current capacity as unofficial American ambassador, and OG Boss (Original Girl Boss), can you cause a different kind of viral spread. You, and others like you who have a global platform, can create positive change through your influence. You've done it already, and for your contributions, I thank you.

I urge you to continue to tell the stories of the unsung and continue to mobilize your peers to do the same. Let's reach deeper into our communities locally to continue the global work of healing by helping to heal our educational systems and underserved neighborhoods. Let's empower those women, Black, Brown, and every other shade, who won't get the opportunity to share their "me too" stories on a national stage but still deserve to be in safe and respectful work environments. Like the civil rights pioneers before us, let's build bridges through meaningful discourse that the children after us can walk across to reach a more integrated and equal America.

I was encouraged when I saw the crowds of women, all around the world, gathered to demonstrate their support of each other at the second annual Women's March. When the first march happened in 2017, I thought it was in response to the election of a president who has been accused of sexual harassment by over a dozen women. Honestly, I didn't expect the movement to continue. I expected that, like most rallies, people would return to their normal lives never to revisit a cause that they were once so passionate about. A second march happened on the anniversary of Mr. Trump's inauguration with even more supporters and more influential voices than the first march. When millions of people across the world came together in their respective communities in peaceful protest in response to George Floyd's death, I watched with optimism for a more equal America and thought to myself, *Oh my god, this is starting to spread!*

We can create our own narrative. We can change the outcome of our own collective and individual stories. I have a stage 4 sense of urgency about my own life. Jasmine and I have attended three funerals in the past two years of either people that we both knew or loved ones of people that we know. Life is not too short. I believe that life is a predetermined amount of time that God gives us to take our best shot at becoming as close as possible to imitating Him. That's not an easy task, and many of us wait far too late to learn that lesson. Each day gives us an opportunity to either choose hate or choose love.

As a morning routine, I've adopted the practice of silent meditation followed by reciting the Peace Prayer of Saint Francis. It says, "Lord, make me an instrument of your peace. Where there is hatred, let me sow love; where there is injury, pardon; where there is doubt, faith; where there is despair, hope; where there is darkness, light; where there is sadness, joy. O divine Master, grant that I may not so much seek to be consoled as to console, to be understood as to understand, to be loved as to love. For it is in giving that we receive, it is in pardoning that we are pardoned, and it is in dying that we are born to eternal life. Amen." This routine enables me to effectively deal with whatever life brings to me that day. I don't handle everything perfectly, but I manage my life better today than I did yesterday.

My experiences have taught me that life isn't fair. People will forever see me as first a Black man and then whatever else comes after in their minds. I'm okay with that. I know that I'm challenged with the task of enlightenment as are many others who happen to have a difference of skin color or difference of sexual orientation, religion, nationality, or whatever it is that makes him or her unique. I know that I can't be a bystander in life, allowing the world to dictate my destiny. I will embrace the man that God has called me to be by learning from my past mistakes and loving the hell out of those in my sphere. I won't keep wearing the albatross of fear, guilt, failure, and rejection. I will keep my eyes lifted toward the heavens from which I gather my strength to grab every blessing that has been carved out for me. I will grab the hands of those following behind me to pull them forward into their destiny. I will use the platform that I have today, pressing toward the platform of tomorrow to reach more people who haven't yet found their power. That is my calling. That is our calling. Let's go get it.

Barrett Blackmon is the author of *Metastatic America*, a book that provides social commentary on the state of race, religion, and culture in the United States as told through his life experiences as a Black health-care executive. Barrett has worked as a health-care administrator in the field of oncology for nearly twenty years and is a fellow in the American College of Healthcare Executives. He is currently a vice president at one of the largest health-care systems in the country.

Having a father who died from cancer and a mother and sister who both battled the disease, he dedicated nearly half of his life to understanding and fighting it. His goal now is to dedicate his time to giving a voice to the often unheard, unseen, and unappreciated.

Barrett has experience in the performing arts, which provided transferable skills for his work in health care. Whether on stage in local performances or acting in front of a camera, Barrett has honed his ability to be comfortable performing or speaking in front of audiences. He is a frequently sought-after presenter to give talks at cancer awareness and community health events.

Barrett has an incredibly supportive wife and three fantastic children. Through his writing and speaking engagements, Barrett plans to highlight social and cultural injustices to spark conversation that helps bring about meaningful and significant change in societies around the world.